Ν. ΙΘΑΚΗ
IS. ITHAKI

Ν. ΑΤΟΚΟΣ
IS. ATOKOS

N

Ν. ΚΕΦΑΛΛΗΝΙΑ
IS. KEFALONIA

GENERAL SUPERVISION: Henriette Metaxas

TRANSLATION FROM THE GREEK : Timothy Cullen

TEXT EDITOR: Yianna Evstathiou-Manolakou

ARTISTIC SUPERVISION: Helena Tzaneka

WORD-PROCESSING, PROOF-READING: Io Yianellis

PHOTOGRAPHS:
George Avgoustinatos (1, 16, 42, 45, 49, 50, 55, 60, 62, 63, 66, 68, 70, 72, 73, 86, 91, 92, 98, 103, 109, 111, 114, 129, 132, 142, 148, 152, 154, 169, 172, 176, 192, 199, 200, 202, 203, 205, 208, 213-216, 218)
Spiros Damoulianos (166, 170)
© P. Dendrinos / Mom. (150)
Nikos Dessilas (115, 128, 207, 221)
Spiros Kapatsoris (178)
Yerasimos Karavias (201, 204, 209)
Theodora Theofilatou (21, 30, 41, 43, 51, 54, 56, 57, 77, 89, 95, 118, 123, 157, 173, 177)
Haralambos Solomos (164)
The archives of: the Corgialenios Historical and Cultural Museum (2, 7, 11, 12, 36, 143, 194, 197), the Ecclesiastical Museum of Ayios Andreas Milapidias (83, 174), the 6th Ephorate of Prehistoric and Classical Antiquities (61, 79, 80, 99, 100, 107, 121, 126, 167), the Kefalonia and Ithaki Natural History Museum (65, 179), the Kefalonian Wine-Growers' Association (35), Lambros Simatos (13, 53, 120, 133)
Publications of: the Kefalonia Historical Archives (9, 10, 76, 124, 162, 168, 177), Spiros Dendrinos (193)
Remaining photographs are from the archives of REITHRON Editions.

MAPS: OKYALOS

COVER DESIGN: Marianna Vallianou

PRODUCTION: TOXO O.E.

PRINTING AND BINDING: A. Petroulakis S.A.

Henriette Metaxas "Discovering … KEFALONIÁ AND ITHÁKI"
© REITHRON Editions

ISBN: 960-87349-2-4

Discovering ...

KEFALONIÁ
AND
ITHÁKI

TRANSLATOR'S NOTE ON THE SPELLING OF GREEK NAMES

Modern Greek place-names have been rendered phonetically as far as possible, with an accent to indicate the syllable to be stressed (e.g. the stress in 'Kefaloniá' falls on the final *a*). Sometimes a form closer to the Greek spelling is added in brackets, to make it easier to read signposts, etc., e.g. Mt. Énos (Aínos). Some names of persons and organizations depart from this system to conform to established usage.

When referring to ancient and medieval Greece, the spellings conform to one of the standard systems used by ancient historians and Byzantinists: so we have Kephallenia, Kephallenians and Kephalos, for example, instead of Kefaloniá, Kefalonians and Kéfalos.

All this may seem unnecessarily confusing, but some compromises had to be made.

Note: *tz* in Greek is pronounced *dz*.

A few Greek words are used in the text without explanation:

iconostasis: the screen in a church separating the sanctuary from the nave. (It also has other meanings, but in this book it is used only in this sense.)

Panayía: the Virgin Mary.

paniyíri: a festival in honour of the patron saint of the local church, with eating, drinking, music and dancing as well as religious services (see p. 177).

Platía: Square.

Theotókos: the Virgin Mary (lit. 'Mother of God').

Every effort has been made to ensure that the information given in this book is accurate at the time of going to press. The author is not responsible for any changes in telephone numbers, opening hours, timetables, etc., etc.

Go for the Blue

GREECE-ITALY

PATRAS-ANCONA in 19 hours
PATRAS-IGOUMENITSA-ANCONA in 21 hours
PATRAS-CORFU-IGOUMENITSA-VENICE
IGOUMENITSA-CORFU-BRINDISI

CRETE NEW!
FROM PIRAEUS
CHANIA in 5 hours and 45'

DODECANESE NEW!
FROM PIRAEUS
KOS-RHODES
& PATMOS-LEROS

CYCLADES
FROM PIRAEUS
PAROS-NAXOS-SANTORINI
SYROS-TINOS-MYCONOS
IOS-AMORGOS-IRAKLIA
SCHINOUSSA-KOUFONISSI

FROM RAFINA
ANDROS-TINOS
MYCONOS-PAROS

IONIAN ISLANDS
FROM PATRAS
CEPHALONIA-ITHACA
CORFU

Blue Star Ferries®
No one gets you there better

CONTENTS

KEFALONIÁ

FACTS ABOUT KEFALONIÁ AND THE KEFALONIANS

8   Dear Reader

13   Geographical position - Size - Population

15   The history of Kefaloniá and its people
       Prehistory
       Historical era

28   The natural environment of Kefaloniá

31   The economy

32   What to buy . . .

34   The Kefalonians

39   Calendar of *paniyiria* and other festivals in the summer months

40   Accommodation and food
       Three Kefalonian recipes from Granny Elefthería

43   Some words of warning

A TOUR OF THE ISLAND

46   Argostóli

56   A tour of the Lássi district

62   Lássi - Livathó district
       (Keramiés - Áyios Andréas Monastery - Castle of St. George [the Kástro])

76   Argostóli - Skála - Póros

91   Póros - Piryí district - Sámi

94   Argostóli - Drongaráti Cave - Sámi - Melissáni Cave -
       Ayía Efimía

108   Ayía Efimía - Mírtos - Ássos - Fiskárdo

124   Argostóli - Thiniá district - Lixoúri

139 Omalá valley - Convent of Áyios Yerásimos

142 The Énos (Aínos) National Park

146 Homer and Homeric Ithaka

ITHÁKI

FACTS ABOUT ITHÁKI AND THE ITHAKANS

153 Geographical position - Size - Population

154 The history of Itháki and its people

A TOUR OF THE ISLAND

162 Vathí

166 Southern Itháki

169 Northern Itháki

GENERAL BACKGROUND INFORMATION

176 Practical information

179 Useful phone numbers

180 e-mail

181 Travel agencies

181 How to get to Kefaloniá and Itháki

182 Inter-island ferries

182 Timetable information

182 Hotels

185 Camping sites in Kefaloniá

186 Books on Kefaloniá in English

187 Index

Dear Reader,

The guidebook you are looking at is the best companion you could have
with you when touring the ancient kingdom of 'wily Odysseus'.
The beautiful scenery and rich cultural traditions of Kefaloniá and Itháki
will certainly cast their spell on you from the moment of your arrival.
Every step you take will make you want to see more of their outstanding
beauty and soak up their magical atmosphere

Early seventeenth-century map of Kefaloniá (Bertius).

Now that you are here – or about to come here – do yourself a favour and allow plenty of time to enjoy the delights of these lovely places. Set out like a new Odysseus, and then perhaps, deep down inside you, you will feel as if you are returning to a long-lost second homeland.

Happy holidays!

Henriette Metaxa

KEFALONIÁ

3   *Satellite photo of Kefaloniá and Itháki.*

FACTS ABOUT KEFALONIÁ AND THE KEFALONIANS

Geographical position - Size - Population

The Ionian Islands are a group of about 330 islands and islets, mostly in the Ionian Sea. The westernmost islet is the most westerly point in Greece. Of the fifteen inhabited islands, the seven biggest are known as the Eptánisa (Heptanese, or the Seven Islands): they are Kérkira (Corfu), Paxí, Lefkáda (Leukas or Santa Maura), Itháki (Ithaka), Kefaloniá, Zákinthos (Zante) and Kíthira (Kythera or Cerigo). They cover a total area of 2,307 sq.km. and have a population of about 200,000.

Kefaloniá lies more or less in the middle of the group and is the furthest away from the mainland. Lefkáda lies to the north, Zákinthos to the south and Itháki to the north-east. Kefaloniá and Itháki are separated by a strait about 22 km. long and 3-4.5 km. wide.

With an area of 781 sq.km., Kefaloniá is the biggest of the Ionian Islands. It is the sixth largest of the Greek islands and is ranked eleventh in size among the thousands of islands in the Mediterranean. Two long peninsulas projecting from the main body of the island give it an unusual shape. The dominant physical feature is Mt. Énos (spelt Aínos), which can be seen from far away in the Ionian Sea and on the mainland: its highest peak is 1,628 m. above sea level. The rest of the island is also mountainous, with peaks of 800-1,100 m. Plains are few and far between, and small in size.

At the 2001 census the population of the island was 36,500. Kefaloniá and Itháki together form the Prefecture of Kefaloniá and Itháki. The capital of the Prefecture and main town of Kefaloniá is Argostóli. For administrative purposes Kefaloniá is divided into seven municipalities and one commune: the Municipalities of Argostóli, Palikí, Livathó, Eliós-Prónni, Sámi, Pílaros and Érissos and the Commune of Omalá.

4   *Vase-painting of the mythical hero Kephalos holding his unerring javelin. Beside him is his hound Lailaps, the swiftest dog in Greece. From an Attic lekythos, c. 480 B.C.*

The history of Kefaloniá and its people

Prehistory

Being quite close to the shores of Akarnanía and the Peloponnese and having a deeply indented coastline with plenty of bays and coves offering a safe anchorage, Kefaloniá was a natural place for early human settlement and the development of civilized communities. The first inhabitants lived in caves in the mountains, while the fertile, verdant plains and the plentiful supply of water from the springs on Mt. Aínos provided ideal conditions for growing crops. The landlocked seas between the Ionian Islands and the mainland, with numerous islets dotted about, encouraged local sailors to venture out of the sheltered bays and made it possible for them to undertake longer boat journeys without much danger, and it was not long before they had crossed the Ionian Sea to southern Italy. Kefaloniá is strategically situated at a crossroads of maritime trade routes between Greece and the West, with harbours that served as supply stations and as safe havens in bad weather. The ruins of ancient temples on the coast dedicated to Poseidon and Apollo, the gods of the sea and the sun, remind us still of that bygone era.

Human habitation on Kefaloniá is attested as far back as the Palaeolithic age (from 40,000 to 10,000 years ago), by finds of stone tools around Fiskárdo, Sámi and Skála. Recent excavations in the Drákena Cave in the Póros gorge have yielded major finds from the Neolithic age and the Early Helladic period (5000-2400 B.C.), including pottery and tools made of stone and bone.

The most important phase in the ancient history of Kefaloniá was the Mycenaean period (1600-1100 B.C.), when Kephallenia, Ithaka and Zakynthos (to give their names in a form more acceptable to classicists), together with the coastlands of the north-western Peloponnese and Aitolo-Akarnanía, belonged to the realm of Odysseus (Ulysses), ruler of the 'proud-hearted Kephallenians'. Traces of Mycenaean settlements have been found at several sites on Kefaloniá, in the areas of Palikí, Kraniá, Livathó, Sámi and Prónni. There are also Mycenaean cemeteries with chamber tombs and tholos ('beehive') tombs in Palikí, Kraniá, Livathó and Eliós. The large Mycenaean tholos tomb at Tzannáta near Póros, discovered during excavations in 1992, is a par-

5

Flint tools of the Final Neolithic from the Drákena Cave in the Póros gorge.

ticularly fine example of the type. On the available archaeological evidence, Kephallenia was unquestionably the centre of the Mycenaean civilization in the islands off western Greece.

Kephallenia was probably associated with the myth of the hero Taphios, son of the sea god Poseidon, who was the first king of the islands off western Greece. His people, the Taphioi or Teleboes, made their living from piracy and were the scourge of the Ionian Sea. After Taphios's death, his son Pterelaos was powerful and bold enough to attack Mycenae itself, the centre of the Mycenaean world.

Another myth tells the story of Kephalos, son of Deioneus, who unwittingly killed his wife Prokris, the daughter of Erechtheus, whereupon he left Athens. After assisting Amphitryon in a campaign against the Taphioi, he became the new king of Kephallenia. Kephalos's grandson was Laertes, father of the wily Odysseus who ruled Homeric Ithaka (see p. 146). Homer uses the term 'Kephallenians' to denote the inhabitants of all the islands ruled by Odysseus, but we do not know the name by which the biggest of the Ionian Islands was called in antiquity. The name Kephallenia was first used by Herodotos in the fifth century B.C., while the geographer Strabo (1st cent. B.C.) tells us that the name Kephallenia was said to be derived from Kephalos.

Historical era

Classical and Hellenistic periods. During the Classical period (5th cent. B.C.) there were four city-states on Kephallenia, each with its fortified acropolis. They were Krane, Pale, Same and Pronnoi, the 'Kephallenian tetrapolis'. The mountains formed natural boundaries between the four cities, which were politically and economically independent (each one had its own coinage, for example) and inveterate rivals.

During the Persian Wars the Kephallenians fought alongside all the other Greeks. In the Peloponnesian War (431-404 B.C.) they gave support to both sides: Pale sent ships to assist Corinth, Sparta's ally, while Krane sided with the Athenians. Pronnoi joined the second Athenian Confederacy when it was formed in 375, and between 374 and 372 the Athenians won over the other three cities by force. In the mid third century B.C. the Kephallenians belonged to the Aetolian League and fought against the Macedonians. In 218 Philip V of Macedon attacked the island with the intention of annexing it, but in the face of heroic resistance by the Palaeans he was forced to withdraw without achieving his object.

Roman period. In 189 B.C. the Romans attacked Kephallenia, because its strategic position in the Ionian Sea gave it a key role to play in their expansionary designs. After a four-month blockade, in which the people of Same put up a valiant defence, the island became a Roman province. Wealthy Romans came to live on the island, as we know from the ruins of their luxury villas found on the east coast. It was during the Roman period that the new city of Panormos was founded at the northern end of the Érissos peninsula, on the site of the village of Fiskárdo. Recent excavations in a large Roman cemetery at Fiskárdo have yielded valuable finds.

Christianity, whose advent signalled the end of the ancient era, was introduced to the islands at the time of the apostles. A German scholar, Professor H. Warnecke, has recently put forward a theory that Melita, the

6

Coins of the four city-states of Classical Kephallenia. Pale: a grain of barley; Pronnoi: a fir cone; Same: an ox; Krane: a ram.

island on which St. Paul was shipwrecked on his way from Crete to Rome (A.D. 59), is to be identified with Kefaloniá and not with Malta. His theory has been widely accepted, and so the Church on Kefaloniá is now classified as one of the apostolic churches. The imposing Early Christian basilica at Fiskárdo and the age-old local traditions testify to the strength of the faith on the island.

Byzantine period. From the fifth century onwards the coastlands and islands of the Ionian Sea were continually ravaged by marauding Vandals from Africa and Goths, and later by Saracen and Slav pirates. In the mid eighth century the Byzantine imperial government created the Theme (administrative district) of Kephallenia, which was a naval command and included all the islands in the Ionian Sea. Kephallenia was the capital of the Theme, which was administered by local noblemen. The purpose of creating the Theme was to control and protect the coastal areas of the Ionian Sea and the southern Adriatic, which were still dangerously exposed to pirate raids. Throughout those centuries living conditions on the islands were very bad, as a result of corrupt government by political adventurers and pillaging by corsairs.

The Byzantine Empire, a synthesis of Roman institutions, Orthodox Christian faith and Greek language and traditions, lasted for well over a thousand years and bequeathed a heritage of flourishing scholarship and cultural attainment which profoundly influenced the Italian Renaissance and hence Western European civilization.

In 1085 the Norman duke Robert Guiscard landed an army in Athéras Bay in an attempt to capture territory from the Byzantines. He died on the island the same year, but the Normans preserved his memory by renaming Panormos as Portus Wiscardi, subsequently corrupted to Fiskárdo.

Following an unwelcome visit in 1103 by soldiers taking part in the First Crusade, who pillaged the island, the Venetians made their appearance and captured the fortress of St. George near Argostóli in 1126. Venice was the up-and-coming new maritime power in the Eastern Mediterranean, and Kefaloniá, the largest of the Ionian Islands, was the most strategically placed

An old map of Kefaloniá (Tommaso Porcacchi).

to control the local shipping routes. Historians have found indications of demographic change on the island at about this time as a result of the havoc wrought by successive invasions and pirate raids.

Frankish period (1185-1485). In 1185, when the Normans were engaged in a large-scale campaign against the Byzantine Empire, a Norman fleet commanded by the freebooter Margaritone captured Kefaloniá, Itháki, Zákinthos and Corfu. Margaritone's occupation did not last long, but from that time on Kefaloniá was never again part of the Byzantine Empire.

When the armies of the Fourth Crusade captured Constantinople in 1204, Kefaloniá was allotted to the Venetians, who appointed another freebooter as its governor. This was Matteo Orsini, Count of Rome, who founded a dynasty that held Kefaloniá (as well as Itháki and Zákinthos) as its own fiefdom under Venetian sovereignty until 1324. During this period piracy was rife in the Ionian Sea. The pirates had their bases on the coasts of Kefaloniá and Itháki, and the strait between the two islands was particularly dangerous. The population of the islands dwindled considerably.

The Orsini were succeeded by the Tocchi, a family that already had fiefdoms in mainland Greece. Carlo Tocco I was one of the most ambitious and powerful rulers in the whole of the Greek East. Under his rule the Kefalonians at last enjoyed a measure of prosperity and well-being. His wife Francesca, an unusually well-educated woman who had adopted some Greek ways, introduced a touch of luxury and better amenities, as well as courtly manners, into his palace in the Castle of St. George.

The Catholic Church made a number of important changes in ecclesiastical affairs. The Orthodox bishop of Kefaloniá was replaced with a Catholic prelate. In the middle of the fifteenth century the Orthodox bishop was reinstated, so that there were two parallel bishoprics, but the animosity between the two churches remained strong in spite of some attempts at rapprochement and co-operation. The dominant features of life during this period were the Vatican's strenuous efforts to impose the Catholic faith on these Orthodox islands in pursuit of its political interests and the harsh treatment of the peasants, who lived in poverty and squalor under the burden of heavy taxation, in stark contrast to the privileged noble families.

Many new Orthodox churches and monasteries with fine painted and sculptural decoration were built between the eleventh and fifteenth centuries, when Kefaloniá was under 'Frankish' rule, testifying to the islanders' deep religious faith and high cultural standards. Unfortunately, few specimens of Byzantine art and architecture have survived on Kefaloniá, because of the frequent earthquakes. Under the Orsini a *praktikón* (register of landed property) of the Catholic diocese of Kefaloniá was drawn up. This valuable document, which still exists, provides a wealth of information about the villages, families, churches and monasteries and about the properties owned by the monasteries. It proves that several of the villages were founded by Italian settlers and named after their founders: for example, Ferendináta and Karoussáta in the Pílaros district were founded respectively by Florentines and by the Caruso family of Naples.

8

Venice in the days when she was 'Queen of the Seas' (1454). The winged lion of St. Mark is the city's emblem.

Turkish period (1479-1481 and 1485-1500). The Turks were masters of Kefaloniá for two brief periods, during which the island suffered appalling destruction and devastation. They had overrun the whole of mainland Greece after capturing Constantinople – for centuries the capital of the Byzantine Empire and the bastion of Western civilization – in 1453.

Venetian period (1500-1797). In 1500 the Venetians captured Kefaloniá with assistance from the Spanish. They retained control for almost three centuries, until 1797, which gave a great boost to the island's prosperity and political stability. The Turks, led by the notorious corsair Khair-ed-din Barbarossa (Redbeard), a renegade Greek, attacked the island in 1537, causing great devastation and taking many prisoners. In another Turkish attack the next year, again probably under the command of Khair-ed-din Barbarossa, 13,000 Kefalonians were carried off by the Turks and sold in the slave markets of North Africa and Constantinople. The important point, however, is that the Ionian Islands did not become part of the Ottoman Empire.

Possession of the strategically-situated Ionian Islands meant that the Venetians, who also ruled Crete and Cyprus, controlled the sea routes used by their merchant ships sailing to and from North Africa. Trade flourished, and Venice, once an unimportant city surrounded by water and without any

9

The Virgin of the Akáthistos Hymn (Stéfanos Tzangarólas, 1700).

agricultural land, developed into one of the richest states in Europe and a great maritime power.

The new social structure of the Ionian Islands was based on the feudal model of Western Europe. The administration was run by Venetian officials based in Corfu. All important decisions were taken in Venice. Each island had its own governor, the Provveditore, working in co-operation with the local aristocracy who owned the land. The names of the noble families were recorded in the so-called 'Golden Book', the *Libro d'oro*. The middle class, composed of well-off merchants and tradesmen, acquired some social influence, while the *popolari* – the lower class of manual workers – were subject to all kinds of obligations. From the seventeenth century the middle class and the *popolari* became more vociferous in their demands for better living conditions and social status and came into open conflict with the ruling class.

10

The Archangel Michael (early 17th cent.). The icon is in the Church of Ayía Marína at Soullári in the Palikí peninsula.

The Castle of St. George, generally known as the Kástro, which had been the capital of Kefaloniá since 1500, was the headquarters of the Venetian administration, whose officials lived there in luxurious *palazzi* and grand houses. Some of the noble families had their homes there as well. The population, which had shrunk alarmingly in the turbulence of the preceding centuries, started to grow rapidly. Settlers arrived with their families from Western Europe and from other Venetian possessions in Greece, as well as thousands of refugees fleeing from the new Turkish overlords of what had been Greek territories. According to official census results, the population of Kefaloniá in the mid seventeenth century was approximately 60,000. Needless to say, the new arrivals brought with them different customs and traditions and a different outlook on life, and so the Byzantine tradition and local customs coexisted with new-fangled ways imported from the West.

The official language was Italian, but Greek remained the language of the people. Not surprisingly, a good many Italian words were assimilated into the language spoken in the Ionian Islands, and the Italian influence is still noticeable in the local dialect today. Here it is worth digressing for a moment to remark that through all the periods of foreign rule in the Heptanese, the other islands and the mainland, the Greeks never lost their sense of national identity. They have always felt that they belonged to a nation with the same ethnic roots, the same language, the same religion, the same gods and holy places in antiquity and, in general, the same customs and traditions. The geographical (and, in the past, political) fragmentation of the Greek homelands has never changed that.

The new social structure, increasing prosperity and Western influence made it possible for more and more young people to go on to higher studies in Western Europe, with many of them going to the famous universities of Venice, Padua and Pisa. Many of the islanders who settled permanently in Italy and France had distinguished careers in the academic world and in the arts or were very successful in business. Those who came back home with a university education and European ideas started schools in the islands, through which they influenced local political, social and cultural developments. Two great names in this context are Vikéntios Damodós, who founded a school at Havriáta in the Palikí peninsula (see p. 134), and the Lihoúdis brothers (see p. 34), who taught for a time at the school in the Kástro.

When the Venetians lost Crete to the Turks in 1669, thousands of Cretan refugees settled in the Ionian Islands. Among them were scholars and scientists, artists and craftsmen working in wood, stone and silver. The magnificent icons and carved wooden altar screens made for Kefalonian churches by Cretans in the seventeenth and eighteenth centuries provide evidence of an artistic 'wind of change' showing traces of Italian Renaissance influence. Among those who contributed to this were artists and craftsmen from the mainland, mostly from Epiros, who came to live on Kefaloniá. Some of the most prominent Cretan painters who worked and taught in the Ionian Islands were Ilías Móskos, Theódoros Poulákis and Stéfanos Tzangarólas. Fine works of art dating from this period are to be seen in various old and new churches on the island.

Hand in hand with the progress of scholarship and art and the growth of trade, poetry and drama came to play a major part in the life of the islands. Following the introduction of Western musical education and opera from Italy, theatres were built and very creditable productions of Italian operas and Greek theatrical works were staged. It was at this time that the foundations were laid of the 'Ionian School', which produced a galaxy of poets headed by Dionísios Solomós (1798-1857) of Zákinthos, the author of the Greek national anthem, subsequently set to music by Nikólaos Mándzaros of Corfu.

In 1757 the Venetian administration decided to move the capital of Kefaloniá from the Kástro to Argostóli, which was the main commercial centre because of its large and very well-protected harbour. Little by little, the inhabitants of the Kástro followed suit.

First French occupation (1797-1799). The French Revolution ended the supremacy of the aristocratic Venetians and brought about a change of political régime in the Ionian Islands. In 1797 Venetian rule collapsed and the islands were occupied by republican France. The arrival of the French forces under the Corsican General Anselmo Gentili was greeted with great rejoicing, for it presaged an end to the privileges of the nobility and the advent of equality for all citizens. One of the first acts of the French after landing on Kefaloniá was to burn the *Libro d'oro* and the standard of St. Mark in the Piazza del Orologio (now Platía Kambánas, 'Bell Square') in Argostóli.

Russo-Turkish intervention. Despite the efforts of the French to improve the quality of life on the islands by opening more schools and founding a National Library and a National Printing House on Corfu, the wind of democracy did not blow for long. The seeds of disenchantment were sown by the new government's fiscal policy and the French treatment of the local people, and this discontent was fomented by the reactionaries. In the autumn of 1798 a Russo-Turkish fleet commanded by Admiral Ushakov wrested the Ionian Islands from the French, with the result that the aristocratic *ancien régime* was restored.

The Septinsular Republic (1800-1807). Under the Treaty of Constantinople (1800) between Russia and Turkey, the Ionian Islands were recognized as an integrated state to be known as the Republic of the United Seven Isles or, more simply, the Septinsular Republic, under the suzerainty of the Sultan of Turkey. This was the first independent Greek state to be created in modern times, with its own constitution and flag. The constitution of 1800, known as the Byzantine Constitution, provided for an oligarchic system of government. Revised constitutions were drawn up in 1803 and 1806, reducing the privileges of the nobility and abolishing hereditary titles, but the oligarchic system was retained.

Second French occupation (1807-1809). The Peace of Tilsit (1807) gave the Ionian Islands to France (now under the First Empire), but her rule lasted for only two years. Tilsit marked the beginning of a new period of obdurate and bloody struggles by the islanders, which continued until the Seven Islands were finally reunited with Greece. Fearing that the islands might be annexed by France, the British imposed a commercial blockade. The islanders, unable to sell their farm produce grown for the British market, appealed to Britain to intervene so that their trade could recover.

British period (1809-1864). Following Napoleon's abdication (1814) and the Treaty of Paris (1815), the Seven Islands were declared a 'unified, free and independent' state to be known as the 'United States of the Ionian Islands', or more simply as the Ionian State, with its capital at Corfu, under the direct and exclusive protection of the United Kingdom. Under the new dispensation the islanders ordered their own affairs, subject to the approval of the Protecting Power, and this régime lasted until the union of the Ionian Islands with Greece in 1864.

As soon as the treaty of 1815 had been signed, the British sent Sir Thomas Maitland out as the first Lord High Commissioner of the Ionian Islands. By means of heavy-handed repression and the use of force, Maitland imposed on the islands the Constitution of 1817, which gave them a parliamentary system of government – on paper, at least – and confirmed the federal structure of the state. In practice, however, all power was in the hands of the 'Lord High', and many of the constitutional rights that the islanders

11

The Áyii Theódori lighthouse on the Lássi peninsula. It was built in the space of two months in 1829 by the then Resident, Charles Napier, to a design by the civil engineer J.P. Kennedy.

had acquired on the formation of the Septinsular Republic were annulled. This régime of independence under Britain's protection was doomed to failure by its very nature.

This awkward situation coincided with the Greek Revolution against the Turks, which had broken out in 1821. The Ionian Islanders were actively involved in the struggle for liberation from Turkish rule. The foremost Kefalonian freedom fighters were the brothers Andréas and Konstandínos Metaxás and Evángelos Panás. British government policy at this time was pro-Turkish, as the Ottoman Empire was seen as a bulwark against the Russians' expansionary designs in south-eastern Europe. Consequently the 'Lords High', seeing the islanders organizing themselves to contribute men and matériel to the War of Independence, took draconian measures to stop them. Greece finally became an independent kingdom in 1830.

One of the most able Residents of Kefaloniá was Charles James Napier (1822-1830), who greatly improved the infrastructure with public works projects such as roads, public buildings and lighthouses: in and around Argostóli he was responsible for modernizing the town plan, constructing new roads and

12

The Napier Gardens in the early nineteenth century.

public buildings, draining the marshes of the Koútavos lagoon, building the Áyii Theódori lighthouse and improving De Bosset's bridge across the bay, while his legacy at Lixoúri includes the Markátos Building and the great lighthouse (34 m. high) on Vardiáni islet. The roads he built made it much easier for goods to be carried between the villages and the ports. Napier was also a staunch supporter of the Greek revolution of 1821 and helped the mainland Greeks as well as the Kefalonians in the War of Independence.

An important event in the history of the Seven Islands was the founding of the Ionian Academy, the first Greek university, at Corfu in 1824. Eminent scholars, scientists and philosophers taught at the Academy, and when it closed down after the union with Greece many of them moved to Athens to teach at the university there.

John Colborn, Lord Seaton, was a progressive 'Lord High' who introduced the freedom of the press in 1848 and permitted the islanders to form political clubs and hold political meetings, which turned out to be fertile seedbeds for the spread of liberal ideas and Greek nationalism. Anti-British feeling was stronger on Kefaloniá than on the other islands and erupted more often. Two of the biggest uprisings were in 1848 (the 'Holy Cross' rebellion) and in 1849 at Skála. Both were put down by the British with heavy loss of life.

13

Emblem designed for the fiftieth anniversary of the union of the Ionian Islands with Greece (1914).

It was at this time, from 1848 to 1864, that the Radical movement made its appearance in the Ionian Islands. Kefaloniá was the cradle of the Radical Party. The most prominent Radicals, such as Ilías Zervós-Iakovátos, Yerásimos Livadás, Iosíf Momferátos and Yeóryios Typáldos-Iakovátos, had studied at universities in Western Europe, from which they had picked up the latest ideas on democratic reform. The Radicals, being a party of the common people with revolutionary aims, gave voice to the Greek people's aspirations for independence and social justice. The Party's primary goal was to unite the Ionian Islands with the rest of Greece. However, opinion in the islands was divided on the question of which course promised the better future: to continue under the British protectorate or to be united with Greece. The Radical

The Radical members of the Ionian Parliament representing Kefaloniá and Itháki: (1) Yerásimos Livadás, (2) Stamátios Pilarinós, (3) Ioánnis Typáldos-Dotorátos, (4) Iosíf Momferátos, (5) Ilías Zervós-Iakovátos, (6) Nathanaíl Domenikínis, (7) Yeóryios Typáldos-Iakovátos, (8) Andréas Karoússos, (9) Tilémachos Paízis, (10) Frangískos Domenikínis.

14

Party wanted union, the Conservative Party supported the British and the Reform Party was in favour of revising the 1817 Constitution, believing that the time was not yet ripe for union with Greece. The majority of the population embarked on a long campaign of resistance against the current political situation, with protest meetings, demonstrations, insurrections and revolutionary articles in the local papers. The British responded with a mailed fist, sending troublemakers to prison and exiling the Radical ringleaders to small, remote islands. In 1858 they sent no less a person than William Gladstone to review the political situation and propose such reforms as he saw fit. However, the Ionian parliament rejected his proposals and continued to press for union with independent Greece.

15

A Kefalonian priest and his wife. Water-colour by the Kefalonian artist Yerásimos Pidzamános (1787-1825).

That cherished goal was eventually attained in 1864. The Ionian parliament was dissolved and the last Lord High Commissioner, Henry Storks, formally ceded the Ionian Islands to the official representative of the Greek government, Thrasívoulos Zaímis. The Ionian State ceased to exist, and since then the fortunes of the islands have been interwoven with those of Greece.

From 1864 to the present day. For most of the nineteenth century and the first half of the twentieth, the political situation in Greece was unstable and the task of building the new state after so many centuries of foreign rule was beset with problems of all kinds. Development was repeatedly held up, first by the Balkan Wars (1912-1914) and then by the two World Wars. Meanwhile the industrial revolution of the nineteenth century had made changes in the traditional agricultural structure of Greek society. After the Asia Minor disaster of 1922 the whole country, and Athens in particular, was flooded with Greek refugees from Turkey, who worked as factory hands. Living conditions were bad for the workers in Athens and the seeds of socialism fell on fertile ground. One of the main exponents of socialist ideology was a Kefalonian, Marínos Antípas (see p. 112).

In the First World War Greece fought on the side of the Allies and won some battles in Macedonia that had a major bearing on the outcome of the war. Greece entered the Second World War on 28th October 1940, when the then prime minister, Ioánnis Metaxás, uttered his famous OXI ('No!') in reply to Mussolini's ultimatum, which was presented in the form of a request to allow the Italian army free passage into and through Greece. The Italian occupation of the Ionian Islands lasted until 1943, when the Germans arrived to take over from them. There ensued one of the most horrific episodes to occur in the Mediterranean theatre of the war. The officers of the Italian Acqui Division on Kefaloniá refused to hand over to their allies, with the result that 5,000 Italian officers and men were slaughtered. Then 3,000 Italian soldiers were killed when the ships taking them to forced labour camps in Germany struck mines. Altogether 10,000 men of the Acqui Division lost their lives. A few managed to escape from Kefaloniá with the help of the islanders.

The years immediately following the German occupation were a grim period in Greek history. The civil war (1944-1947), which arose from fears of a Communist takeover of Greece and an expansion of Soviet influence, split the country right down the middle, with villages and even families divided against themselves. Since 1974 Greece has been a republic, and it is now a member of the European Union and of the so-called Eurozone.

In August 1953 Zákinthos, Itháki and Kefaloniá were struck by a very severe earthquake and a series of aftershocks. Prompt assistance was provided by many European countries and the long process of recovery was undertaken mainly by the islanders themselves. Eventually, after decades of unremitting hard work and self-sacrifice, all the villages and towns were reconstructed. In Kefaloniá whole villages were rebuilt in different locations, sometimes several kilometres away from their original sites and usually nearer the sea. Nowadays all buildings have to conform to strict anti-seismic specifications and no building may have more than three storeys.

16

The modern town of Argostóli.

The natural environment of Kefaloniá

17

Almond blossom.

Kefaloniá is a mountainous island of outstanding natural beauty, with an abundance of vegetation but little flat country. The highest mountain is Mt. Énos (Aínos), of which the highest peak is called Megálos Sorós (1,628 m.). The coastline is deeply indented and its 250-kilometre length is full of contrasts, with long sandy beaches, steep cliffs and pretty little coves.

18

Lavatera, which grows to a height of three metres.

Most of the island is typical karst country, consisting of limestone honeycombed with subterranean streams. Caves, potholes and chasms are to be found all over the island.

The marine swallow-holes (*katavóthres*) just north of Argostóli are a unique phenomenon: there the seawater plunges into holes by the shore and makes its way through rifts in the limestone until it reappears on the other side of the island, at the brackish springs of Karavómilos and the Melissáni Cave, near Sámi (see p.102).

The flora is very varied, with the number of different species running into

19

Vitex agnus-castus (chaste tree).

Thyme. 20

21

Cyclamen.

22

Cistus (rock-rose). A low shrub that flourishes in the lowlands and the maquis.

23

Euphorbia on Mt. Énos.

hundreds. The Énos National Park (see p. 142) is of particular interest for the endemic species of fir, *Abies cephalonica*, that grows in its forests. Many of the plants typical of Kefaloniá have survived on the mountain in isolation, including some endemic species that are not found in any other country.

The commonest coniferous trees on the island are pines, cypresses and firs. Other trees include olives, planes (near streams and springs), poplars and kermes oaks (holly-oaks). Various saline plants grow near the sea. In the lowlands and on the lower mountainsides, which stretch almost from the seashore to about 800 m. above sea level, the Mediterranean maquis has supplanted the Mediterranean forests, which have disappeared over the centuries through the effects of agriculture and stock-breeding. Here we find tough-leaved evergreen shrubs such as lentisks, Spanish broom, myrtles, oleanders and arbutus (strawberry-tree), as well as heather. Of the many culinary and medicinal herbs that grow on the island, sage, mint, chamomile, valerian, oregano, thyme, rosemary and fennel are a representative selection. In spring, when the hundreds of different wild flowers are in bloom, Kefaloniá is a riot of colour. Irises, anemones, violets, poppies, crocuses, marigolds, daisies, various kinds of euphorbia (spurge) and mallows are just a few of the wild flowers that grow in profusion. Orchards, too, contribute to this vernal pageant: the almond blossom, which comes in January and February, signals the advent of spring.

It is worth mentioning that some typical Kefalonian plants and trees have actually been introduced from other continents: the eucalyptus from Australia, the prickly pear from America and the agave from Africa.

24   25

Wild flowers.   *Giant fennel.*

Bougainvillea, which adds a characteristic splash of purple or red to the walls of many local houses, was introduced from Brazil in the eighteenth century.

26

A swallow feeding its young.

The fauna is almost equally varied. There are game birds such as quails and partridges, predators such as owls and many kinds of raptors, including some rare species, and any number of different warblers and other songbirds. The migrants that visit the Ionian Islands gather in large numbers in the wetlands of the Koútavos lagoon near Argostóli and Livádi in the Palikí peninsula. Small mammals and reptiles are to be found all over the island. Dolphins are often seen offshore, and the rocky stretches of coast are a habitat of the rare Mediterranean monk seal (*Monachus monachus*), of which there are only a few thousand left in the whole of the Mediterranean. The beaches of southern Kefaloniá are breeding-places of another endangered species, the loggerhead sea turtle (*Caretta caretta*), which come in summer to lay their eggs in the sand.

27

Black-figure amphora with a painting of the olive harvest (530-510 B.C.).

According to Greek mythology, the goddess Athena introduced the olive tree into Greece and taught the Greeks how to cultivate it. In antiquity the olive was held sacred and olive-growing had an important place in the Greek economy. The oil was stored in large amphorae and much of it was exported. The ancient Greeks identified over sixty medicinal properties of the olive, and sprigs of olive leaves were given as prizes to the winners of athletic and literary competitions. To this day, an olive branch is the symbol of peace.

Olives are widely grown throughout the Mediterranean basin and the olive is one of the commonest trees on Kefaloniá. Ancient trees with massive, strikingly gnarled trunks are to be found all over the island. In autumn and winter the olive harvest is one of the main agricultural occupations. Kefalonian olive oil is considered to be of exceptionally high quality. Olive oil is an essential ingredient of modern Greek cookery and its beneficial effects on the human constitution are universally recognized.

28

Olives.

The economy

The Mediterranean climate, stunningly beautiful scenery and innumerable beaches are some of the factors behind the steady growth of tourism, which is now a major item in the local economy. Tourism, bringing foreigners to the island, is seen not only as a source of revenue but also as a continuation of the age-old tradition of keeping in touch with the outside world. The other main economic activities are commerce, agriculture, stockbreeding, fishing and shipping. Olive oil, wine, honey and dairy produce are some of the staple products of the farming sector, known for their high quality, and exports of fish from the fish farms around the coast are increasing steadily.

29

Black-figure kylix (shallow goblet) with a painting of an open-air drinking party (late 6th cent. B.C.).

In ancient Greece, wine was associated with the cult of the god Dionysos. It was a standard accompaniment to meals (though hardly ever drunk neat), and ancient Greek drinking-parties have given us the word *symposium.* Wine intended for sale was kept in earthenware storage jars (amphorae or *pithoi*) glazed on the inside to prevent it from going sour while being transported, often by sea to distant countries. The modern Greeks still regard wine in modest quantities as a healthy source of energy. Farm workers usually take a little wine with them to the fields to drink with their lunch. Greeks always have something to eat with their wine.

Vines have been grown on Kefaloniá from time immemorial. According to ancient myth, the hero Kephalos brought a vine with him from his homeland of Attica. The variety of grape most widely cultivated in the central uplands is called Robóla: it produces a high-quality white wine sold as 'Robóla of Cephalonia'. Other wines are also made from local varieties of grape.

30

Robóla grapes.

What to buy....

31

Mándoles, perhaps the most typical local item of confectionery.

32

33

Olive oil.

Thyme honey.

Small works of art, pottery, souvenirs, etc.

34

Robóla, the famous wine of Kefaloniá.

35

The Kefalonians

The alternation of rugged crags and gentle scenery in the Kefalonian landscape is reflected in the character of the people. Kefalonians tend to be headstrong, austere and somewhat brusque in their manner, but at the same time they are kind-hearted and quick-witted, with a love of music and dancing. Wit, stubbornness and progressive ideas are their salient characteristics. Born into a race of merchants and seafarers, they are to be found all over the globe, enterprising and successful in whatever they do. It is worth quoting a passage from *Journey to Greece*, a book written about 200 years ago by the Sicilian historian and economist Saverio Scrofani, who makes some perceptive observations on the Kefalonian character:

The character of the Cephalonian is shaped by the island's healthy climate and favourable natural environment.... He is frugal, energetic, shrewd and ambitious.... Although they live only a day's journey away from Corfu and Zakynthos, they are quite unlike the inhabitants of those two islands. Vivacious, witty, quick-witted (or should I say crafty?) and mercenary, they are quite prepared to leave their native land for twenty years if need be. While the Zakynthians and Corfiots squander their fortunes at home, the Cephalonians cross the oceans, settling everywhere, founding colonies on the Black Sea, in Asia Minor and in Egypt, and then come back home with their earnings to spend their old age with their families.... The Cephalonians are perhaps the only race on earth whom Nature created to live everywhere.... You would think they were inhabitants of a great capital city rather than of a small island in the Ionian Sea. In our own time they have a Regent in Sicily, a teacher in Brazil, a great general and a famous architect in Russia.... There are only 60,000 of them, but they have more than two hundred big ships and five thousand small ones at sea. The Adriatic, the Archipelago and the Black Sea are full of Cephalonian ships, some of which go as far as America and India. Nor are they any less enterprising in their native land....

Go-ahead Kefalonians who have made successful careers in the academic world, the sciences and the arts, commerce and other branches of human activity are to be found today in every continent. They have been doing this for centuries, and many of them rose to positions of prominence. In the eighteenth century the brothers Ioanníkios and Sofrónios Lihoúdis, who had studied at Venice and Padua Universities and whose names were known to the readers of learned journals, founded the Slavic-Greek-Latin Academy in Moscow, which was the first university in Russia. This was at the time of the Russian Renaissance under Tsar Peter the Great. Graduates of the Academy went on to hold important positions in Russia.

A typical instance of Kefalonian enterprise, this time connected with maritime exploits, is the case of Apóstolos Valeriános Fokás from the village of Valeriáno, who became an admiral in the Spanish navy. In Spain he was known as Juan de Fuca, and that is the form of his name that has gone down in history. From the fourteenth to the seventeenth century it was quite usual for Greek seamen to serve under foreign flags, in warships as well as merchantmen, and from 1590 to 1592 De Fuca was leading an exploratory expedition for Philip II of Spain in search of a sea passage between the Atlantic and the Pacific. Setting out from Mexico (then a Spanish colony), he sailed up the west coast of America until he reached the spot where

Vancouver now stands, in Canada. Subsequently the channel between Vancouver Island and the coast of Washington state was named Juan de Fuca Strait in his honour. So it came about that the Kefalonian Juan de Fuca was the first European to go so far north up the west coast of America, exploring by land and sea.

Another well-travelled Kefalonian was Konstandínos Yerákis, born at the Kástro in the mid seventeenth century. Born into a poor family, he went to sea at the age of twelve. Many years later, by which time he had acquired an education, spoke several languages and was a veteran of various hair-raising adventures at sea, he met in Asia a Siamese ambassador who was impressed by him and gave him an introduction to King Narai of Siam (Thailand). In time Yerákis rose to be Regent of that far-off country and founded schools, seminaries, colleges of higher education and an observatory. He was also the architect of three treaties between the King of Siam and Louis XIV of France concerning the organization of the Siamese army along European lines and the introduction of Christianity. Yerákis's genius and practical abilities were acknowledged even by his enemies. He met his death together with the royal family in 1688, when a high-ranking official seized the Siamese throne with the support of foreign powers (the Dutch, Portuguese and Ottoman Turks) who feared that his reforms were harming their commercial interests in the region.

In the nineteenth century the Kefalonians had the largest merchant fleet in the Ionian Islands, and even today many of the big Greek shipping companies were founded by Kefalonians. For centuries Kefalonian ships roved the world's oceans. Hundreds of Kefalonian communities abroad were established by sailors who left their ships and decided to spend the rest of their lives where they were, sometimes in the most remote places. Many of these tiny colonies mushroomed as they were joined by emigrants in the

36

The Kefalonian-owned three-master Áyios Nikólaos (early 19th cent.).

37

Vespers at the Monastery of the Theotókos Átrou.

nineteenth and twentieth centuries: a wave of emigration set in from about 1800, first to Constantinople and the countries round the Black Sea, later to America, Africa and Australia, and in the twentieth century to northern Europe. After the 1953 earthquakes Kefalonians left the ruins of their homes in their thousands and the population shrank from about 70,000 to about 25,000. For years nothing could stem this exodus, but since 1980 the growth of tourism has brought a gradual increase in the population. Many of those who still live abroad have built holiday homes in their old villages so as not to lose touch with their roots.

Characteristic features of Kefalonian culture are polyphonic singing and the local dances, a mixture of traditional music and dancing with a noticeable dash of Western influence. There are dozens of choirs on the island and elsewhere keeping up the tradition of part-singing, much of their repertoire consisting of traditional *kantádes* and *ariéttes*. The most typical local dances are the Kefalonian version of the *bállos* (with its flamboyant figures and fast steps), the *mérmingas*, *divarítikos* and *manéttas*.

38

Preparing for the paniyíri of the Blessed Virgin on 8th September at the Átros Monastery. For many years now the goat soup served here has been cooked in the traditional way by Mr. Víronas Fourniótis.

39

Carnival time: dancing quadrilles in the main square at Póros. The dancers are wearing fancy dress with the usual accoutrements such as helmets, scarves, costume jewellery, wristwatches and so on.

Many Kefalonians are named after the island's patron saint, St. Gerásimos (pronounced Yerásimos). The diminutive forms of the name are Yerasimákis, Mákis, Memás and (on Itháki) Mássos. Abroad, the name is often changed to Gerry. The feminine equivalent is Yerasimoúla or Mémi. Greeks automatically assume that anyone called Yerásimos is from

40

The Argostóli town band in Platía Valliánou during the parade to celebrate the union of the Ionian Islands with Greece on 21st May.

41

The Municipality of Pílaros dance group.

Kefaloniá and will expect him to be a resourceful individualist: there are any number of well-known anecdotes about men with that name who are sharp-witted and well-travelled Kefalonians.

Kefalonians are rightly proud of their beautiful island. So long as you respect the people and their environment, you can expect to enjoy their unfeigned hospitality and the traditional way of life on the island. A good way of meeting the local people and finding out about some of the traditions is to go to a *paniyíri* or other festival.

42

Calendar of *paniyíria** and other festivals in the summer months

May

1 Taxiarchs (Archangels Michael and Gabriel) .... Perahóri (Itháki)
21 SS Constantine and Helena .... Karavádos
21 Anniversary of the union ....Parades in the main squares of Argostóli,
   of the Ionian Islands with Greece   Lixoúri and Vathí (Itháki)

June

1 Panayía Diótissa .... Días islet
24 St. John .... Tzannáta, Kióni (Itháki)
30 The Twelve Apostles .... Havdáta

July

11 St. Euphemia (Efimía) .... Ayía Efimía
17 St. Marina .... Vlaháta, Exoyí (Itháki)
20 Prophet Elias (Elijah) .... Razáta, Frangáta, Kaminaráta, Kióni (Itháki)
25 St. Anne .... Lakíthra
26 St. Paraskeví .... Troianáta
27 St. Panteleimon .... Kondogouráta, Pouláta
End of July, Wine festival .... Perahóri (Itháki)

August

6 Metamórfosi Sotíros (Transfiguration) .... Kalligáta, Póros, Travliáta,
                                                              Áyios Nikólaos, Stavrós (Itháki)
Last Sunday before 15th .... Ayía Iríni
15 Dormition of the Virgin .... Markópoulo, Aryínia, Pástra, Lixoúri,
                                                              Havriáta, Damoulianáta,
                                                              Platrithiás (Itháki), Anoyí (Itháki)
16 St. Gerásimos: .... Áyios Yerásimos Convent, Skála
16 Robóla festival .... Valsamáta

First weekend after 16th, Robóla festival .... Frangáta
Mid August, Wine festival .... Manzavináta
23 Octave of the Dormition .... Panayía Agrilíon Monastery, Kechriónos Convent
29 St. John .... Radzaklí

September

8 Nativity of the Virgin .... Dilináta, Átros Monastery, Makriótika,
                                                              Paliohérsou Monastery, Katharón Monastery (Itháki)
14 Exaltation of the Holy Cross .... Estavroménou Monastery at Pessáda,
                                                              Kipouréon Monastery
24 Panayía Drapaniótissa .... Argostóli
25 St. John .... Sarláta

October

20 St. Gerásimos .... Áyios Yerásimos Convent
26 St. Demetrios .... Lixoúri
28 National holiday .... Parades in the main squares of Argostóli,
   ('Ohi Day', 1940)   Lixoúri and Vathí (Itháki)

* *Paniyíria* are usually held on the evening before the feast-day.

Accommodation and food

Kefaloniá is a large island and it takes time to explore it thoroughly. For your overnight stays you have a choice of hotels of all classes, pensions, rented apartments and guesthouses in all parts of the island. Advance booking is essential in summer, especially in July and August. At other times of year it is easy to find accommodation of the standard you want and the prices are lower than in high season. Every room should have a notice on the back of the door showing the price and listing the services provided, with the official rubber stamp of the G.N.T.O. There are also two camping sites on the island, one at Argostóli and the other at Sámi. 'Free' camping is forbidden under Greek law.

43

Fiskárdo.

Kefaloniá has a wide variety of restaurants and traditional tavernas, including fish restaurants. Most of them offer traditional dishes such as Kefalonian *kreatópita* (meat pie), *skordaliá* (garlic purée, also called *aliáda* locally), *moussaká*, *pastítsio* (macaroni pie), *stifádo* (a spicy stew of beef, rabbit, etc., with shallots), *youvétsi* (braised meat with minestra), as well as good local wine and delicious Kefalonian desserts such as *amigdalópita* and *karidópita* (strudels with almonds and walnuts respectively).

Here are three traditional Kefalonian recipes.

Three Kefalonian recipes from Granny Elefthería

Granny Elefthería has lived all her life in a village on Kefaloniá. The recipes that follow are the ones she has been using for the last seventy years, learnt from her mother and grandmother. Good luck!

Kreatópita (meat pie)

Kreatópita is a traditional dish eaten in most Kefalonian homes and often served on name-days (which take the place of birthdays in Greece). *Kreatópita* made with goat's meat used to be served at village *paniyíria* after the traditional goat soup.

For a large baking tin (approx. 35×40 cm.) you will need:
1½ kg. meat (beef and pork)
1 onion
1 head of garlic
parsley
marjoram

1 tbsp. tomato purée diluted with a little water
or 200 gm. (½ packet) concentrated tomato juice
2 cups water
2 cups long-grain rice
1 cup grated cheese
1½ cups olive oil or
olive press oil
½ cup white wine
1 tsp. sugar
1 tsp. salt
pepper
grated nutmeg
For the pastry:
¾ kg. plain flour
1 egg
½ cup white wine
a little warm water
a pinch of salt

44

Wash the meat, dice it into small cubes and mix it well with the other ingredients in a large mixing bowl. The parsley, garlic and onion should be finely chopped. Lastly, add the rice and water.

For the pastry: Put the flour into a mixing bowl, reserving 1 cupful to flour the board when rolling the pastry. Add the other ingredients and knead the mixture thoroughly. Add warm water, a little at a time, until the dough is the right consistency to be kneaded without sticking to the bowl. Take a bit more than half the dough and roll it out to the desired shape and size on a floured surface. Grease the baking tin and line the bottom and sides with the sheet of pastry, which should overlap the edge of the tin all round. Roll out the rest of the dough for the piecrust. Fill the pie with the meat mixture and cover with the lid, folding the overlapping edges back over the lid and pinching them lightly together to seal the join. Oil the top lightly and prick it here and there with a fork. If you like, you can brush the top with egg yolk for a glossy finish. If you are unsure about your abilities as a pastrycook, you can use ready-made frozen pastry.

Preheat the oven to 180°C and bake for about 1½ hours. If you find it is getting brown too quickly, cover with aluminium foil.

Skordaliá with cod

Skordaliá (garlic purée, also called aliáda locally)
is traditionally made with a pestle and mortar,
the mortar being made of metal or stone.

Ingredients for six portions:
2 kg. potatoes
1 slab salted cod
2 tbsp. coarse salt
1 head of garlic
(or more, to taste)
2 cups stock from
the boiled cod
½ cup lemon juice
2-3 cups olive oil
or olive press oil

46

45

Soak the fish overnight in plenty of cold water. Boil the potatoes with their skins on. Cut off two pieces of cod and boil them to make the stock. Pound the garlic and salt in the mortar. Peel the potatoes, add 3 or 4 of them to the mixture while still hot and pound to a purée. Transfer the purée to a bowl. Pound the rest of the potatoes and add to the garlic mixture. Add the fish stock, lemon juice and oil in that order, a little at a time, until the purée has the consistency of a dip.

Cut the cod into portions, coat with a batter of flour, water and salt (no egg) and fry. Make sure the fat is hot when the fish is put in, then fry over moderate heat for 5 minutes on each side. Beetroot and boiled courgettes go very well with this dish.

Amigdalópita

Amigdalópita is a cake soaked in syrup. In the old days there was an almond tree in the garden of every Kefalonian house, and they are still widely grown on the island. Almonds keep very well, so housewives always had the ingredients at hand to make a traditional sweetmeat for special occasions.

For a large cake tin you will need:
10 eggs
10 tbsp. breadcrumbs (crushed rusks)
10 tbsp. ground almonds* (not too fine)
7 tbsp. sugar
a little cinnamon
* The same cake made with walnuts instead of almonds is called *karidópita*.

For the syrup:

1½ cups cold water
5 tbsp. sugar
a few leaves of scented
geranium or a little brandy
grated rind of 1 lemon
1 stick of cinnamon
3 cloves

47

Mix the egg yolks with the sugar, using a wooden spoon. Stir in the breadcrumbs and grated almonds, a spoonful at a time, and finally add the cinnamon. Beat the egg whites until they are stiff and fold them into the mixture carefully, again using a wooden spoon. Turn the mixture out into a greased cake tin. Preheat the oven to 200°C and bake for about 30 minutes. Test by sticking a cake tester or steel knitting needle into the cake: if it comes out dry, the cake is ready.

The syrup:

Prepare the syrup before the cake. Put all the ingredients into a saucepan, bring to the boil and simmer gently for 10 minutes. Remove the spices and leave to cool. Spread the syrup evenly over the hot *amigdalópita* with a spoon: it should all be absorbed.

Some words of warning

Engineering roads through the mountains is by no means a straightforward matter. Sharp bends and steep gradients often make it impossible to see far ahead when driving. In general the roads on Kefaloniá are well signed, but not every hazard is marked and you have to be prepared for potholes, fallen rocks or a sudden narrowing of the road. Be careful when you see a sign warning of an intersection ahead, because the intersection will usually be only a little way beyond the sign. If you want to look at the view, park at the edge of the road where you will not cause an obstruction, and never on a bend. Most of the little wayside shrines you will see have been put up after a road accident at that spot: let them serve as reminders of the dangers lurking on the roads.

You should be on the alert at all times for sheep and goats, which you may find walking along the road, crossing the road or even sleeping in the middle of the road.

If you rent a motorbike or scooter, you should be particularly careful on bends, because there may be loose gravel at the edge of the road causing you to skid and fall off. Dress sensibly when riding a motorbike: if you can't hire a crash helmet, at least wear a cap and clothes that protect you against sunburn, and glasses or goggles to keep the insects out of your eyes.

Even if you are an experienced swimmer, it can be dangerous to venture far offshore. Stinging jellyfish are an infrequent hazard, but it is a good idea to take a tube of anti-sting cream when you go to the beach. When in the sea at a remote beach, avoid putting your foot down on rocks or where the seabed is stony: you may tread on a sea urchin, and if you do your foot will be painful for a few days and there may be some swelling.

Stray dogs roam everywhere. If a dog comes towards you, its intentions are usually friendly, but if you're not sure, don't pat or stroke it. If you give food to a stray dog, it will think it has found a friend and may well follow you around wherever you go.

48

Ayía Efimía.

A TOUR OF THE ISLAND

Argostóli

Argostóli, the main town of Kefaloniá, is the administrative and commercial capital of the Prefecture of Kefaloniá and Itháki, with a population of about 9,000. It is situated on an arm of the Gulf of Argostóli, the fourth biggest natural harbour in Greece. Facing it across the harbour are Mt. Evmorfía (1,035 m.) and Mt. Évyeros (823 m.). To the east one can see the hill crowned by the Kástro (Castle of St. George), with Mt. Énos rising behind it.

The new Argostóli is the intellectual, cultural and commercial centre of the island. A walk around the town will show you how the Kefalonians live today: they belong to an island community that has learnt to live with globalization while still retaining its own traditions and distinctive characteristics. You can hardly fail to be captivated by the friendliness of the people, their love of singing and dancing, their sense of humour, the special greetings and wishes for every occasion and the traditional festivals.

The stone-arched Drápanos bridge, 900 m. long, is one of the few old structures that survived the 1953 earthquakes. It connects Argostóli with the opposite side of the bay and separates the harbour from the Koútavos lagoon. The original wooden bridge was built in 1813 by the Resident of Kefaloniá, Charles Philippe De Bosset, who saw that it was needed because Argostóli was virtually cut off from most of the island. The only way to get to it from the other side of the bay was either by boat or by travelling right round the Koútavos lagoon, which was then a dangerous swamp. The town council objected to the ambitious plan of building the bridge, partly because of the cost but also because it would expose the inhabitants to the risk of raids by bandits from the villages across the bay. However, De Bosset was not a man to be trifled with and the bridge was built in two weeks! The townspeople were delighted and the opposition abated. Thereupon De Bosset immediately

Panoramic view of Argostóli.

laid the foundations of the stone bridge, which was completed by Charles Napier, De Bosset's successor. The obelisk in the sea about half-way along has an inscription commemorating De Bosset as the initiator of the project and giving the date of construction (1813). With a little bit of luck you may be able to see loggerhead sea turtles (*Caretta caretta*) swimming near the bridge. These creatures mate in early summer in the shallows of the bay, and

The obelisk half-way along the Drápanos bridge, with Argostóli in the background.

52

View of Argostóli by the English artist Joseph Cartwright (1789-1829).

The name **'Argostóli'** is known from before 1500, but there is no satisfactory explanation of its derivation and meaning. In 1757 the Venetians decided to move the capital from the Kástro to the then insignificant village of Argostóli, and after that it developed rapidly. Its sheltered harbour provided a safe anchorage for the large Kefalonian merchant fleet and for foreign ships as well. Trade flourished and the town grew steadily. New public buildings and handsome private houses were built, in which Venetian baroque elements were combined with traditional Kefalonian features. Humbler houses, shops and workshops, churches with tall bell-towers, a municipal concert hall and theatre, piazzas and public gardens completed the picture of a romantic Heptanesian town. After the 1953 earthquakes Argostóli was rebuilt in modern style.

53

A nineteenth-century town house.

Platía Valliánou.

54

the females then swim to the beaches near Cape Moúnda, at the south-eastern tip of the island, to lay their eggs in the sand.

Near the starting-point of the Drápanos bridge is the Panayía Sissiótissa, a historic church that was rebuilt after the earthquakes. Its iconostasis (altar screen) was moved here from the Church of Áyios Nikólaos in the Kástro. The church stands at the southernmost end of the commercial centre of Argostóli with its shops, the vegetable market and the fish market to which the fishermen bring their catches after a night's fishing, tying their boats up to bollards on the pebbled quayside. North of the fish market is the yacht harbour, then the Port Authority, the offices of the Greek National Tourist Organization (G.N.T.O.) and the berths of the car-ferries for Killíni and Lixoúri. Further along the quayside stands the bust of Níkos Kavvadías (1910-1975), the poet of the sea, who was a sailor himself. The recurrent themes of Kavvadías's poems are travel, nostalgia, love, life and death. He was nicknamed Marabou (which was the title of his first published collection) and many of his poems, set to music, are well-known songs with an enduring appeal.

55

Níkos Kavvadías, 'the poet of the sea'.

Inland from the Port Authority is Platía Valliánou, the main square, surrounded by cafés, patisseries and restaurants, with the statue of the national benefactor Panayís Valliános dominating the scene. In summer the square is closed to traffic in the evenings and the whole expanse is full of people socializing and enjoying themselves. The Prefecture (Nomarchía), the Town Hall (Dimarchío), the Kéfalos Municipal Theatre, the Corgialenios Library, the Corgialenios Historical and Cultural Museum and the other museums are south of the square.

West of Platía Valliánou are the Napier Gardens, commemorating the fruitful period when the philhellene Charles Napier was the British Resident of Kefaloniá. Fifty metres from the gate of the gardens is the Harokópio Workshop (60, P. Harokópou St.), where you can buy traditional embroidered work done to designs copied from old embroideries in the Corgialenios Historical and Cultural Museum. The workshop also takes special orders. A little way beyond that is the one and only open-air summer cinema on the island: here you can enjoy good films, many of them old classics, in a flowery garden beneath the star-studded sky. Foreign films are not dubbed into Greek but are shown in the original language with Greek subtitles.

Going south from Platía Valliánou, you come soon to the beginning of the Lithóstroto (the 'cobbled street'), still the main shopping street of Argostóli as it has always been. Not far along it is the Church of Áyios Spirídon, which has an eighteenth-century gilded iconostasis of carved wood and some fine modern wall-paintings done in Byzantine style. One of the paintings on the north wall depicts Theodora, the dynamic ninth-century

The **Kéfalos** Municipal Theatre occupies the same site as the old theatre, which was inaugurated in 1859 with a production of Verdi's *La Traviata* and was destroyed in a bombing raid in 1943. In the nineteenth century it put on popular Italian operas and plays by Greek dramatists, and it was a very flourishing institution. The new theatre is a spacious, modern building used for plays, opera, ballet and concerts, and as a conference hall. In winter it also serves as a cinema. Art exhibitions, mainly of work by Kefalonian artists, are held on the ground floor.

56

A scene from a production by the Argostóli Amateur Dramatic Society at the Kéfalos Municipal Theatre.

57

Platía Kambánas.

58

The Radicals' Monument.

Byzantine Empress, holding an icon The church, which is open every day, is the starting-point of the annual procession held on 12th August in memory of the 1953 earthquakes. Further along the Lithóstroto is the Catholic Church of Áyios Nikólaos, and fifty metres beyond that is the rebuilt campanile with the clock in Platía Kambánas ('Bell Square'), which was called the Piazza del Orologio in the Venetian period. The coffeehouse on the ground floor of the campanile has old photographs of Argostóli hanging on the walls. From the top of the campanile there is a panoramic view of the town.

Running north-west from Platía Valliánou is the broad avenue called Leofóros ton Rizospastón ('Avenue of the Radicals'), lined with palm trees and oleanders. In this road are the Argostóli Philharmonic School and one of the few old mansions to have survived the earthquakes. At the far end stands the Radicals' Monument by the Kefalonian sculptor Yeóryios Bonános, a monument to the islanders' struggle for liberty (on the Radical movement see p. 25). Here a ceremony is held every year on 21st May to commemorate the union of the Ionian Islands with Greece in 1864.

The road beyond the monument takes you past the Ionian Islands Merchant Marine Academy and the municipal swimming pool. Below the swimming pool is the fishing port.

59

At the edge of the town, on the shore of the Koútavos lagoon, is a sports complex comprising the football ground, tennis and basketball courts and the Andónis Trítsis Gymnasium. The area around the lagoon is a park closed to traffic, inhabited by swans, wild ducks and other birds.

The Drápanos cemetery on the other side of the bay, on the road to Lixoúri, has served the town since the nineteenth century. Next to it are the Catholic and Protestant cemeteries.

Statue of the late Andónis Trítsis, a former government minister and mayor of Athens, by the Kefalonian sculptor and painter Dioníssis Kaloyerátos, who lives and works in Athens.

60

The pedestrianized promenade along the waterfront.

Museums in and around Argostóli

● **Argostóli Archaeological Museum** (G. Vergotí St.). The new exhibition rooms contain archaeological finds (vases, tools, coins, sculptures, personal ornaments, mosaics, etc.) from the Palaeolithic through to the Roman period, illustrating the island's long history and the development of its culture. One whole room is given over to the Mycenaean period, the most important in Kefaloniá's ancient history, with finds from the cemeteries excavated at Kokoláta, Mazarakáta, Lakíthra, Metaxáta, Kondoyenáda and Póros. The exhibits are accom-

61

Gold double-headed axe from the Mycenaean tomb at Tzannáta.

panied by photographs and information boards. In front of the museum stands a statue of Ilías Tsitsélis, a historian and folklorist from Lixoúri.
Opening hours: Tuesday-Sunday 08:30-15:00. Closed on Mondays and public holidays.

● **Corgialenios Library** (12, Ilía Zervoú St.). Founded under the terms of a bequest by Marínos Corgialenios (Koryalénios), a local benefactor, in 1924. The building was destroyed by the 1953 earthquakes and reconstructed in 1963 as it had been before. It contains about 60,000 books and is one of the biggest libraries in Greece. About half the books, in Greek and other languages, date from the nineteenth century or earli-

62

The Corgialenios Library.

er. The oldest printed book is the lexicon called *Souda* or *Suidas*, published in 1499. There is a special section of the library devoted to Kefalonian literature and newspapers and periodicals from the Ionian Islands, mostly from Kefaloniá. The main collection has books of all kinds as well as a considerable number of manuscripts, including some of Byzantine music, and the personal papers of the Kefalonian writers Bábis Ánninos and Mikélis Ávlihos. The oldest manuscript is a twelfth-century Gospel book. The main room, where the books are kept, also serves as a reading room and is sometimes used for lectures. Books may not be borrowed. Byzantine icons from the personal collections of Panayótis Harokópos and Panayís Valliános are also exhibited in the library.
Opening hours: Monday-Saturday 08:00-21:00. Closed on Sundays and public holidays.

- **Corgialenios Historical and Cultural Museum**. On the ground floor of the Corgialenios Library. The museum has an extensive collection giving a comprehensive picture of life on Kefaloniá in bygone ages, displayed in several rooms with a total floor area of 300 sq.m. The exhibits include old lace, embroideries and ladies' dresses, traditional local costumes, household utensils and tools, old furniture, photographs of Kefaloniá before the earthquakes, old prints, maps and paintings, old icons, sacred relics and carved wooden iconostases. One room is a reconstruction of a nineteenth-century bedroom. Books and pamphlets on Kefalonian history, published by the museum itself, are on sale in the entrance hall.

A nineteenth-century bedroom.

Opening hours: Monday-Saturday 09:00-14:00. Closed on Sundays and public holidays.

- **Fokás-Kosmetátos Museum** (1, P. Valliánou St.). This small new museum is on the ground floor of the Fokás-Kosmetátos Foundation, which occupies what used to be the family home. The house was rebuilt after the 1953 earthquakes on a smaller scale than before. The private collection of the three Fokás-Kosmetátos brothers contains lithographs of scenes in the Ionian Islands and elsewhere in Greece and old coins from various parts of the Mediterranean basin.

The flag of the Septinsular Republic (1800), whose central feature was the Venetian winged lion. Between the pages of the closed book held by the lion are seven arrows, one for each island.

Opening hours: Monday-Saturday 09:00-14:00. Closed on Sundays and public holidays.

- **Museum of Radio and Telecommunications Equipment** (a private museum belonging to Mr. Harálambos Makrís). The exhibits are in excellent condition and visitors are permitted to switch the machines on and off. Visits by prior arrangement only, tel. 2671 022 679.

- **Kefaloniá and Itháki Natural History Museum at Davgáta.** To reach the museum, cross the Drápanos bridge, follow the Lixoúri road and turn right to Davgáta. The museum is clearly signposted in the village. The collection was put together recently by a team of scientists, all experts in their various fields, and provides a wealth of information about the flora and fauna of Kefaloniá. The building also houses the Centre for Environmental Studies, which has a library and a small laboratory.

Viola cephalonica, an endemic plant of Mt. Énos.

Opening hours: Monday-Friday 09:00-13:30, 18:00-20:00. Saturday and Sunday 09:00-13:30. Closed on public holidays.

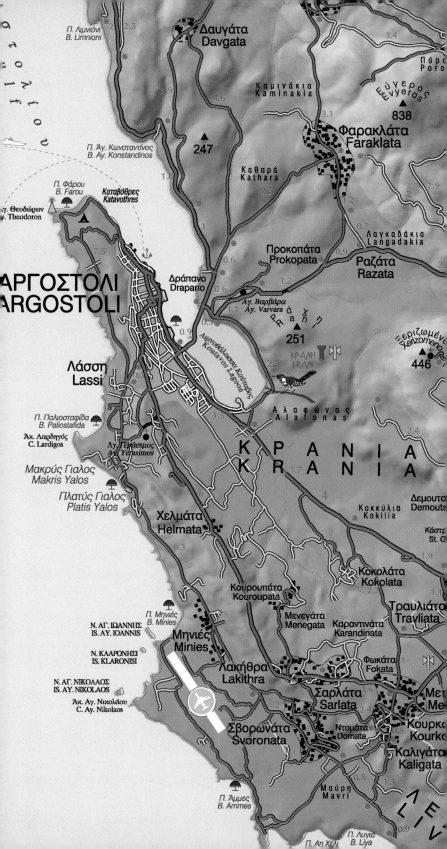

A tour of the Lássi district

A trip round the coast of the Lássi peninsula, north-west of Argostóli, makes an enjoyable outing through pleasantly varied scenery, with fine views of the Palikí peninsula to the west, and is a popular walk with the townspeople, especially at sunset. Lássi used to be a farming area, but since 1980 it has developed as a summer resort with very good tourist facilities, a perfect place for a relaxed and relaxing holiday.

Near the entrance to Argostóli's natural harbour are the famous **Katavóthres** (swallow-holes), a remarkable geological phenomenon, where the seawater disappears into large holes at various points along the shore. Where the water went from there remained an unsolved mystery until 1963, when a team of geologists poured a quantity of uranin, a fluorescent dyestuff, into the swallow-holes. Two weeks later traces of uranin reappeared at several places near Sámi: at the springs of Karavómilos, at Frídi, at Ayía Efimía and in the Melissáni lake cave. The experiment proved that the water travels 15 kilometres underground through rifts in the limestone. By the time it reaches the east coast and re-enters the sea it is brackish, because it mixes with subterranean streams of fresh water along the way. In the nineteenth century a mill powered by the natural flow of water was built at *Katavóthres*, and it was later adapted for use as a small hydroelectric generating plant. The building has been restored since the earthquakes and is now a coffee-house.

After *Katavóthres*, at **Fanári** beach, is a camping site. At the tip of the rocks stands the elegant Áyii Theódori lighthouse marking the entrance to the harbour: it is a low rotunda with an outer colonnade of Doric columns,

Tourkopódaro beach on the Lássi peninsula. 66

originally built in 1829 by the then Resident, Charles Napier, and reconstructed after the 1953 earthquakes to a less elaborate design. This is an ideal place to stand and watch the sunset.

Shortly after the lighthouse there is a turning signposted to the Monument to the Fallen Italians (Monumento Caduti Italiani), which stands on a low hill. It was erected in memory of the ten thousand men of the Italian army's Acqui Division, based on Kefaloniá, who lost their lives in the vicious fighting between the Germans and Italians on Kefaloniá in 1943. The hilltop offers a panoramic view.

After a few kilometres the main road arrives at the Lássi tourist resort, and from Faraó Hill you can return to Argostóli.

If instead you carry on along the main road, you come soon to the two splendid beaches of the Lássi area, **Platís Yalós** and **Makrís Yalós**. Both are 'blue flag' beaches, having met the strict international standards for cleanliness, swimmers' safety and watersports facilities. Watersports are available at Makrís Yalós.

The Lássi district boasts the biggest hotels

67

The Katavóthres *(swallow-holes).*

68

Sunset at the Áyii Theódori lighthouse.

on the island, with swimming pools and sports facilities. The restaurants and tavernas there serve traditional Kefalonian dishes, fresh fish and Chinese and Italian food as well. Some of the hotels and restaurants organize 'Greek evenings' with a band, dancing and the traditional Heptanesian part-songs called *kantádes*. Then there are nightclubs and discos where the dancing goes on all night.

69

The Monumento Caduti Italiani. Ceremonies are held regularly in memory of the fallen Italians, attended by the President of Italy

A small turning to the left off the main Lássi road brings you to the **Cave of St. Gerásimos,** where the saint lived as a hermit before founding the monastery at Omalá. There is now a small chapel in front of the cave.

If you make your base at Argostóli or Lássi, you will be ideally placed for day trips to the many interesting sights and good beaches that lie within a relatively small radius.

To return to Argostóli, go back past Faraó Hill, so named after a place of entertainment that existed there long ago. From there the road takes you downhill to the town's main square.

70

Platís Yalós beach.

Walks:
• **Around the town of Argostóli,** as described on pp. 50-60. Time: 1½ hrs.

• **Round the Lássi peninsula:** *Katavóthres*, Áyii Theódori lighthouse, Monument to the Fallen Italians and back into the town from Faraó Hill. Time: 2 hrs.

• A walk affording panoramic views over Argostóli and Lássi at the same time. Starting from the Monument to the Fallen Italians, follow the dirt road

71

southwards along the crest of the hill. After 25 mins., when you come to the first house on the left, you have a choice: (a) Take the dirt road to the right, which brings you down through the olive-groves to Lássi, or (b) Go straight on and after 100 m. turn left: this brings you to the centre of Argostóli. Time from the monument to Lássi or Argostóli: 1 hr.

Useful phone numbers

• Police Station: 2671 022 200
• Traffic Police: 2671 023 226
• Fire Brigade: 199
• Port Authority: 2671 022 224
• Hospital: 2671 024 641
• Post Office: 2671 022 312
• Town Hall: 2671 022 230

• Taxis: 2671 022 700 / 2671 024 305 / 2671 028 545
• Bus Station: 2671 023 364

For tourist information
• G.N.T.O: 2671 022 248
• Tourist Police: 2671 022 815

Kalámia beach.

Lássi - Livathó district

(Keramiés - Áyios Andréas Monastery - Castle of St. George [the Kástro])

The road running south from Lássi takes you to the airport and the Livathó district, which extends southwards from Argostóli and the Lássi peninsula and is one of the most beautiful parts of the island, with lovely scenery and pretty villages. Before the airport, at **Miniés** on the main road, you may be able to visit the Gentilini winery, the first small winery to be established on the island, founded in 1984 by the Kosmetátos family to produce fine wines. Most of its output consists of Robóla wine. Open to the public on Tuesdays, Thursdays and Saturdays, 17:30 till sunset.

The Livathó district, with its many beaches and secluded coves, is an ideal place for a summer holiday. The majestic Énos (Aínos) range towers above it to the north-east and forms the natural boundary of the district, while the Castle of St. George, a relic of the centuries of Venetian rule, dominates the scene at a lower level. In spring and summer the wild flowers turn the whole landscape into a vast garden. Olive-groves, extensive orchards, vineyards, vegetable and flower gardens and well-kept villages with attractive churches complete the picture. There are plenty of hotels and guesthouses throughout the district, especially in the seaside villages. Mycenaean cemeteries have been excavated near Kokoláta, Metaxáta, Lakíthra and Mazarakáta.

The attractive villages of **Svoronáta**, **Sarláta**, **Domáta** and **Kalligáta**, with their narrow alleyways and old houses of the landowning gentry, lie amid orange and olive-groves, with sweeping views over the sea. Nearby are the popular beaches of **Ámmes**, **Ávithos** and **Ái-Hélis**.

Not far from the beach at Ávithos lies the islet of **Días,** where in antiquity there was an altar of Zeus (Dias) exactly opposite the altar of Zeus on the peak of Mt. Énos. Under the British protectorate Días was used as a place of exile for refractory churchmen. A flight of a hundred steps carved out of the rock lead from the little jetty on Días to the chapel of the Panayía Vlahernón (or Panayía Diótissa), which celebrates its patronal feast on 2nd July. An excursion to the islet is run on that day.

The churches at Domáta and Kalligáta have old gilded iconostases of carved wood, dating from the early nineteenth century, and fine icons.

The village of **Kourkoumeláta** was entirely rebuilt after the 1953 earthquakes with funds donated by the great benefactor Yeóryios Vergotís. New roads were built and it was the first place on the island to have electricity after Argostóli and Sámi. Kourkoumeláta is a gem of a village, with attractive houses and clean and tidy streets and public spaces.

The next village after Kourkoumeláta is **Metaxáta**, well situated with

74

The old path from Svoronáta to Sarláta.

75

Wrought-iron gate at Metaxáta.

views of the mountain, the Livathó plain and the sea. Here, in a fine Neoclassical building, there is a cultural centre serving Metaxáta and the surrounding villages, where exhibitions, concerts and lectures are held. The centre was donated by the Vergotís family, which has owned a flourishing

76

Detail of painting of the Twelve Great Feasts (Crucifixion - Entry into Jerusalem - Ascension) in the Church of the Panayía at Domáta.

77

The Neoclassical cultural centre at Metaxáta.

shipping business for hundreds of years and has been a generous benefactor to Greece and to Kefaloniá: among other things, the Merchant Marine Academy, the football stadium, the music school and the Argostóli Philharmonic School were all built with funds donated by the Vergotís family.

A bust of Lord Byron stands in the little square at the top of the village. Byron spent a few months at Metaxáta in 1823 before going to Mesolónghi. The famous poet's arrival on Kefaloniá with his suite of attendants was a great event for all the Greeks involved in the revolution. He had been sent to Greece by the London Greek Committee, bringing arms, medicines and a large sum of money to assist the Greeks in their struggle against the Turks. His few months' stay on the island gave him a chance to form a better assessment of the complex situation in Greece. His death at Mesolónghi in 1824 was a great shock to the Greeks and the rest of the world, because he had come to be seen as a symbol of Philhellenism and of the support given by all civilized peoples to the Greek struggle for national liberation.

78

Portrait of Lord Byron wearing Greek costume of the time of the War of Independence.

Another philhellene who lived in the Livathó district in the early twentieth century was the Dutchman Adriaan Goekoop, looking for evidence of Homer's Ithaka on Itháki and Kefaloniá. It was his belief that the centre of Homeric Ithaka, as described in the *Odyssey*, was in the area round the Castle of St. George. He published his theory in 1907 in

Mycenaean krater (mixing bowl for wine and water) from Lakíthra (c. 1100 B.C.).

79

Excavations at Mycenaean cemeteries at Metaxáta, Lakíthra and Mazarakáta, in use during the Late Mycenaean period (c. 1350 - c. 1050 B.C.), have brought to light personal effects, weapons, jewellery (made with semi-precious stones), amber, glass paste and clay vases that were deposited with the bodies as grave goods, to accompany them to the underworld. About 300 m. south-east of Metaxáta, at a spot called **Halikerá**, Spyros Marinátos and Pétros Kalligás excavated Mycenaean chamber tombs that were found to contain a large number of vases and small artefacts, as well as cult objects ranging in date from the Protogeometric to the Roman period.

At the south end of the village of **Lakíthra** Professor Marinátos discovered some Mycenaean chamber tombs that yielded a rich haul of grave goods. The finds from the Lakíthra cemetery – the richest Mycenaean burial ground so far excavated in Kefaloniá – amounted to about four hundred vases and numerous smaller objects. A representative selection of the vases is on display in the Argostóli Archaeological Museum.

The large cemetery at **Mazarakáta**, about 500 m. south-east of the village, was excavated by De Bosset when he was the Resident of Kefaloniá (1810-1814), then by Panayótis Kavvadías in 1889 and 1908-1909, and again by Marinátos in 1951. The excavations brought to light a great number of Mycenaean vases and small artefacts, of which some are in the Argostóli Archaeological Museum and some in the National Archaeological Museum in Athens, while some were taken to Switzerland by De Bosset and are now in the Neuchâtel Museum.

Earlier graves (c. 1700 B.C.), which were probably in use until the Mycenaean period, have been found at **Kokoláta**.

If you are looking for archaeological sites you may need to ask the way in the nearby villages, because they are not always well signposted.

80

Gold necklace from Lakíthra (c. 1100 B.C.).

Excavating at Mazarakáta in 1908.

French, under the title *Ithaque la Grande*. Much of his personal fortune was spent on the excavations conducted in the Livathó district by Kavvadías and Marinátos. It is interesting to note that his grandson, Cees Goekoop, published a book in Dutch on the same subject in 1990.

At **Lakíthra**, a large village west of Metaxáta that used to be the capital of the Livathó district, there is a spot called Kallithéa from which, as its name implies (Kallithéa means 'Good View'), there are superb views to be had over the whole of Livathó, with Días islet just offshore and Zákinthos in the distance. There is also a crag called 'Byron's rock', where the poet used to sit and write poetry while contemplating the surrounding countryside. The road leading on from Lakíthra to Kombothekráta takes you back to Lássi and Argostóli.

After Metaxáta you have a choice of routes: **(1)** straight on towards the Convent of Áyios Andréas Milapidiás and the Castle of St. George, or **(2)** right towards Spartiá.

A. Route 1. Beyond Metaxáta the road takes you to the historic **Convent of Áyios Andréas Milapidiás**, founded in the thirteenth century. A reliquary in the new church contains the sole of St. Andrew's foot. The old church (built c. 1600) was reconstructed by the army after the 1953 earthquakes and is now used as an ecclesiastical museum. In it there are superb frescoes ranging in date

Plaque on the rock at Lakíthra where Byron used to sit and write poetry inspired by the surrounding countryside. The inscription is a translation of Byron's words, 'If I am a poet, the air of Greece has made me one.'

83

The interior of the old katholikon (conventual church) of the Convent of Áyios Andréas Milapidiás.

from the fifteenth to the eighteenth century, an early seventeenth-century iconostasis and some noteworthy icons by eminent icon-painters of the Postbyzantine period, including Theódoros Poulákis, Stéfanos Tzangarólas, Stéfanos Krassás and Athanásios Ánninos. The gold-embroidered sakkos (a vestment like an alb or a dalmatic) made for Bishop Agápios Lovérdos of Kefaloniá in 1721 is considered to be one of the finest embroideries in the world.

Near the convent, on the other side of the road, is the little village of **Mazarakáta** with its important archaeological site.

For the **Castle of St. George** (the Kástro), turn left at the intersection in **Travliáta** and then immediately right by the plane tree. The road up to the village of **Kástro** and the castle is lined with agaves (century plants, or American aloes), which produce a single flower stem several metres high just once in the plant's lifetime, after many years.

The Castle of St. George, also known as the Castle of Kefaloniá (Kástro Kefaloniás), stands on a hilltop about 7 km. south-east of Argostóli at an altitude of 320 m.

The panoramic view from the Kástro, down over the sea and Argostóli and up to Mt. Énos, gives a good overall picture of the region, with old churches and campaniles recalling the bygone glories of the historic area

The **Kástro** excellent strategic position gave the Venetians control of the southern part of the island, Argostóli harbour and the sea between Kefaloniá and Zákinthos.

The hill was probably first fortified in the Byzantine period. The Orsini and Tocchi (1195-1483) enlarged the Byzantine fortress and used it as an administrative centre and military headquarters: it was then that the town outside the walls (the *borgo* or, in Greek, *boúrgo*) was built. In the two brief periods of Turkish occupation (1479-1481 and 1485-1500) the castle was repaired after being damaged in the 1469 earthquake and the fortifications were strengthened.

In 1500 the Venetians, assisted by the Spanish, besieged the Turks in the castle and forced them to surrender after three months. They then set about rebuilding and reinforcing the walls. The outer wall, which follows the contours of the hilltop and has three bastions, encloses an irregular polygonal enceinte with a perimeter of 600 m. and an area of 16,000 sq.m. The original form of the gatehouse, now mostly in ruins, has been thoroughly obscured by later alterations and accretions. In the enceinte the Venetians put up various buildings, such as administrative offices, residences for the Provveditore and his councillors, barrack blocks, the garrison headquarters, storehouses and water cisterns. The local population, including the Kefalonian nobility, lived in the *borgo*, where there were Orthodox and Catholic churches, schools (often staffed by distinguished teachers) and some grand houses. The Kástro was the island's administrative and ecclesiastical centre from 1500 until 1757, when the Venetians decided to move the capital to Argostóli, then an insignificant village called Porto de la Cephalonia, to facilitate commercial development. Thereafter the castle and the *borgo* fell into decay.

Under the British protectorate (1815-1864) several of the buildings in the Kástro were repaired and altered for the use of the garrison. The 1953 earthquakes seriously damaged the Kástro, which is now covered by the 'Kastron Periplous' programme for the improvement of the site as a whole.

84

A print of the Castle of St. George (the Kástro) (J. Peeters, 1685).

surrounding the castle. Outside the castle gate there is a bust of Iosíf Momferátos, who in 1850 was elected one of the Radical members of the Ionian parliament in Corfu (see p. 26).

B. Route 2. To go to the **Áno Livathó** district, turn right just after Metaxáta. **Keramiés** is the headquarters of the Municipality of Livathó, which has its offices in a carefully restored house belonging to the Valliános family. Panayís Valliános was a national benefactor whose generosity paid for the school at Keramiés, vocational training schools at Argostóli and Lixoúri and the National Library in Athens, among other things. The countryside around the small villages of **Klísmata** and **Koriánna** is ideal for walking.

Spartiá and **Pessáda** are two villages with a great seafaring tradition, which brought them considerable prosperity in the nineteenth century. In the old days the villagers of the Livathó district used to send their greetings to ships passing offshore by signalling with sun-reflectors, and the ships always signalled back. Spartiá was the home village of Evángelos Panás, a ship's captain who commanded the Kefalonian contingent that routed the Turks at the battle of Lála on the mainland in the War of Independence. Below the village there is a sheltered cove and a good beach where boats can be hired. The view over Lourdás Bay and up to Mt. Énos is fantastic. In the middle of the village there is an unusual museum called the House of the Owls and Hedgehogs, which is devoted exclusively to those two creatures: in summer it is open from 18:00 to 21:00 every day except Monday.

Pessáda has a picturesque little harbour from which there is a twice-daily ferry service to Zákinthos in summer. There are several small, secluded sandy beaches near the village, and the whole of this stretch of coast is good for fishing. The Kefalonian Game Farm at Pessáda, run by Níkos Sklavoúnos, is the biggest game farm in Greece: here pheasants, partridges

and quails are reared for hunters who come from all over Greece to shoot them. The Hartouliáris winery at Pessáda has a visitors' cellar where you can taste the wines and buy the products of your choice (open daily, 10:00-20:00).

From Pessáda follow the road through vineyards and olive-groves to **Dorizáta** and on to **Karavádos**, the next village. The Church of SS Constantine and Helena at Karavádos has been rebuilt exactly as it was before 1953. The exterior restoration work, the relief decoration in the interior and the seven wall-paintings are by the Kefalonian sculptor and painter Yerásimos Kaloyerátos, who lives and works at nearby Mazarakáta. From Karavádos a road runs down to the sea at **Áyios Thomás**,

85

The Church of SS Constantine and Helena at Karavádos.

The Castle of St. George (the Kástro).   86

View over southern Kefaloniá from the Castle of St. George.   87

where there are small coves with sandy beaches. The sunset seen from here is a magnificent spectacle.

Not far beyond Karavádos you meet the main road from Argostóli to Póros at a T-junction. To return to Argostóli turn left; for the south-eastern part of the island turn right.

Walks: • Airport - Ámmes beach - Svoronáta - Airport. Take the road that
strikes off to the left just before the airport gate and walk south along the coast with the airport behind you. At the Irina Hotel turn left for Svoronáta. At the intersection in Svoronáta village turn left, then left again at the intersection after leaving the village, and so back to the airport. Time: 2 hrs.
• **Keramiés - Koriánna - Spartiá - Keramiés.** Leave Keramiés by the road leading to Spartiá and take the minor road off to the right signposted to Koriánna and Klísmata. In Koriánna turn left and continue along the road to Spartiá. In the middle of Spartiá leave the church to your right and following the road, keeping left wherever you have a choice. To get back to Keramiés, turn left after leaving Spartiá. Time: 1½ hrs. If you want to go on to Pessáda, go past the church in the middle of Spartiá and turn right at the House of the Owls and Hedgehogs (which has a picture of an owl on the wall). After 200 metres you come to an intersection where you turn left, and follow the road through vineyards and olive-groves to Pessáda. There you should take the first turning to the left and then turn right at the stop sign. To go on down to Pessáda harbour, turn right at the intersection where there is a signpost to 'Argostóli 13'. Time from Keramiés to Pessáda harbour (one way) 2½ hrs.
• **Svoronáta - Domáta - Kalligáta - Kourkoumeláta - Svoronáta.** Follow the road uphill from Svoronáta to Kalligáta and Kourkoumeláta. There is a café at Kourkoumeláta with a good view. Time: 1½ hrs. (round trip).

88

The Convent of Áyios Andréas Milapidiás.

89

Ávithos beach and the islet of Días.

Useful phone numbers

- Argostóli Police Station: 2671 022 200
- Fire Brigade: 199
- Argostóli Hospital: 2671 024 641
- Karavádos Doctor's Surgery: 2671 069 387
- Keramiés Doctor's Surgery: 2671 069 101
- Keramiés Town Hall: 2671 068 232
- Taxis: 2671 028 545 / 2671 022 700 / 2671 024 305

For tourist information
- G.N.T.O.: 2671 022 248
- Keramiés Town Hall: 2671 068 040

The bell-tower of the ruined Church of Áyios Spirídon at the southern edge of Kástro village.

Argostóli - Lourdáta - Kateliós - Skála - Póros

The villages on the main road from Argostóli to Póros lie at an altitude of about 250 m. in the district known as **Ikosimía** ('Twenty-one'). The foothills of Mt.

The beach at Lourdás Bay.

Énos, above and behind the villages, are good bird-watching country. From **Moussáta** a minor road runs down to the sea at **Trapezáki**, where there is a lovely beach with a stand of pine trees offering welcome shade in the heat of the summer.

At **Vlaháta** a turning off to the right leads to the seaside village of **Lourdáta**. The beautiful, curving, sandy beach of **Lourdás Bay** – one of the finest beaches on the island – makes this a very popular spot with holidaymakers and there has been a lot of tourist development. Watersports facilities are available and there is also a riding school that arranges horseback treks up Mt. Énos and in the Livathó district. There are plenty of holiday apartments to let, as well as newly-built guesthouses with modern amenities, nestling among the greenery with good views across the sea to Zákinthos. The coastal strip near Lourdáta is very fertile and has long been known for the excellent vegetables of all kinds produced in its market gardens; in the past, bananas were grown here on a large scale. Near the village square stands the chapel of Ayía Paraskeví, with eighteenth-century wall-paintings.

Soon after **Simotáta**, going south-east along the main road from Vlaháta, a turning to the right leads to the Síssia Monastery (Monastery of the Panayía Sissíon) near the sea. The name Síssia is a corruption of Assisi. Tradition has it that the monastery was founded by St. Francis of Assisi himself, the protector of animals, birds and the world of nature, though others say merely that it was founded by Franciscans in the thirteenth century. Be that as it

93

Detail of the iconostasis at the Síssia Monastery.

may, under the name of Santa Maria di Assisi it was one of the Catholic monasteries already in existence at the beginning of the Venetian period, and as such it received preferential treatment from the Venetian authorities in the Kástro. For a time it was actually exempt from taxation. Precisely when it became an Orthodox monastery is not known. In 1676 the Venetians instituted an annual procession from the Síssia Monastery to the Kástro (then still the capital) on the feast of St. Mark as a token of respect for the 'Most Serene Republic' of Venice (*La Serenissima*, as the Venetians liked to call their home country). Oddly enough, what had started as an obligation imposed on the monastery eventually became established as a religious custom, and the icon of the Virgin Mary is still carried in procession from the monastery to the village of Kástro, a distance of twelve kilometres, on Low Sunday (the first Sunday after Easter) every year. The icon is kept in the Church of the Evangelístria at Kástro for three weeks before being carried back to the monastery in procession on the fourth Sunday after Easter. The monastery was completely destroyed by the 1953 earthquakes and was rebuilt a little further up the hillside. The most valuable treasure in its possession is the icon of the Virgin of the Akáthistos Hymn (Panayía tou Akathístou) painted in 1700 by the Cretan priest and icon-painter Stéfanos Tzangarólas, which is kept in the ecclesiastical museum of the Convent of Áyios Andréas Milapidiás.

After the turning to the Síssia Monastery the main road continues south-eastward towards the **Eliós** district, which is full of picturesque villages set among olive-groves, vineyards, orchards and market gardens. The district is named after the mythical hero Eleios, who was a son of the king of Elis and an ally of Kephalos.

About 1 km. beyond **Platiés** the road forks and you have a choice of routes: **(1)** the right (southerly) fork takes you through some of the Eliós villages to Skála, from where you can continue round the coast to Póros; **(2)** the left (northerly) fork is the main road to Markópoulo, Tzannáta and Póros.

A. Route **1.** The first villages you come to in the plain of Eliós are **Valeriáno** and **Hionáta**. From Valeriáno a minor road runs south-west and makes a circuit through **Thirámona** and **Mavráta** before rejoining the main road a little further on. From Thirámona a pleasant walk through the trees and shrubs and down the steep path at **Skalí** brings you to the sea at the lovely beach of **Koróni**, with other, smaller beaches nearby. There are more good beaches below Mavráta.

94

House at Hionáta.

Near **Mavráta**, at a place called Kotrónia just south-east of the village, there is a small Mycenaean tholos tomb. Finds from there are on display in the Argostóli Archaeological Museum.

On the seabed off Mavráta the wreck of the British submarine H.M.S. *Perseus* was found recently. When the submarine hit a mine and sank in 1941 there was just one survivor, a man called John Capes, who swam ashore and spent several months on Kefaloniá (then under Italian occupation) before escaping with the help of the islanders.

While at Mavráta you may like to visit the Yannikóstas Metaxás winery, where you can enjoy a wine-tasting session in pleasant surroundings, learn about the history of the estate and the secrets of wine-making and buy the wines of your choice. Open to visitors daily, 10:00-18:00 (in August, 10:30-20:30).

Just before the turning off the Skála road to Kateliós you will see a small building which is the Kateliós Environmental and Cultural Centre. The Centre is mainly concerned with the conservation of the marine environment, and it has a permanent exhibition of photographs.

The right fork takes you down to **Káto Kateliós**, a friendly little village whose inhabitants have always made a living by fishing and farming. It has a long, beautiful beach, with the result that much of the flat land in the vicinity – once all farmland – is now occupied by modern tourist facilities, with tavernas along the seashore and round the small fishing harbour. In the old days the men of this district used to leave from this harbour to find work on the big farms in the Peloponnese.

As you drive on towards Skála from Kateliós you can see **Cape Moúnda** ahead of you in the distance. From **Radzaklí** a minor road leads down to **Potamákia** and **Kamínia**, where there are long sandy beaches with warm shallow water. It is to these beaches, which extend for miles towards Cape Moúnda, that the loggerhead sea turtles (*Caretta caretta*) come from thousands of miles away to lay their eggs in the sand. The rare Mediterranean

95

The small fishing harbour at Káto Kateliós.

monk seal (*Monachus monachus*) is sometimes found in the sea caves along this stretch of coast.

Skála, near the southernmost tip of the island, is the most highly developed tourist resort in the Municipality of Eliós-Prónni, thanks to its long, beautiful, well-organized beach and its crystal-clear water. Modern hotels have been built in the flat coastal strip, and holidaymakers come in their thousands. Towards sunset they emerge from their hotel rooms to take their *vólta* or evening stroll in the main street and the village square, where there are numerous tavernas, bars, coffee-bars and souvenir shops. The village is separated from the beach by a stand of pine trees, which offers relief from the sun and adds to the beauty of the beach. For those who want to explore the smaller beaches and secluded coves along the coast, boats, pedalos and canoes can be hired on the beach, and there is also a scuba diving

96

A loggerhead sea turtle laying her eggs.

Caretta caretta is the only species of sea turtle that breeds in the Mediterranean. These large, primeval creatures can be seen in summer off the south coast of Kefaloniá, when the females swim ashore at night to lay their eggs on the long beaches, having mated in the waters of the Gulf of Argostóli. They simply deposit their eggs on the beach, cover them with sand and then swim away. In the course of the summer each female lays about a hundred eggs in different nests. After about 55 days of incubation in the hot sand the baby turtles hatch out and make straight for the sea. Many of them fail to survive because they make tasty morsels for hungry sea birds, but the species is also endangered by the human presence on the beach and in the sea, not only at Moúnda but elsewhere in Greece as well, especially Laganás Bay on Zákinthos and Mavrovoúni and Valtáki in the southern Peloponnese. Speedboats are a hazard in the sea and beach umbrellas can wreck the clutches of eggs in the sand. Even plastic bags in the *sea*

97

A newly-hatched baby turtle heads for the sea.

can be a danger, because the turtles mistake them for the jellyfish on which they feed. And the lights of the hotels sometimes confuse the baby turtles, causing them to crawl inland instead of down to the sea. Teams of biologists visit the Moúnda area regularly to observe the turtles and record the whereabouts of the nests, as the females always return to the same beach year after year.

The beach at Skála.

Detail of the mosaic floor of the Roman villa just outside Skála.

school. A romantic walk along the beach under the full moon on a summer's night is an experience never to be forgotten.

A path leading out of the village near the sea, sign-posted 'Roman villa', takes you to a small olive-grove where the ruins of a Roman villa were discovered in 1957. Parts of the mosaic floors survive in a good state of preservation. The villa has been dated to the second century A.D. and appears to have been burnt down in the fourth century. The mosaic in the first room depicts Envy as a young man being attacked by two pairs of wild animals. In the second room we see three animals (a wild boar, a bull and a ram) ready to be sacrificed. The mosaics have decorative frames with geometric designs. *Opening hours: Tuesday-Sunday 08:30-15:00. Closed on Mondays and public holidays.*

North of Skála, near the chapel of Áyios Yeóryios on the coast road to Póros, are the ruins of an ancient temple, one of the earliest Doric temples of the Archaic period in Greece (6th cent. B.C.), which was dedicated either to Apollo or to Poseidon. It was part of an enclosed sanctuary that also included a stoa (colonnaded gallery) south of the temple and was a cult centre mainly for seamen who passed that way. Blocks of stone from the ancient temple were used in the construction of the chapel of Áyios Yeóryios. From Skála

Foundations of the Archaic temple near the chapel of Áyios Yeóryios, north of Skála.

the road follows a scenic route near the sea all the way to **Póros** (see below).

B. Route 2. The upper road from the fork after Platiés takes you through **Atsoupádes** to **Markópoulo,** a village famous for the harmless snakes with a cross-shaped mark on the head which appear in early August near the Church of the Panayía Lakouvárda (or Panayía Fidoússa) and disappear after 15th August, the feast of the Dormition (Assumption) of the Blessed Virgin. According to a legend recounted by the older inhabitants, the phenomenon originated when the convent that used to stand on the site of the present church was raided by a pirate ship and the nuns were turned into snakes to keep them out of the pirates' clutches. Every year large numbers of devout churchgoers – and tourists too, of course – come to the church on 14th August, the day of the *paniyíri*, to witness the event. The pilgrims handle the reptiles quite fearlessly and call them 'Our Lady's snakes': they are held to bring good luck. It is said that they never appeared in the grim years of the occupation during World War II, nor in 1953, the year of the earthquakes. The same phenomenon is celebrated in a similar way at the nearby mountain village of **Aryínia**, on the edge of the Énos National Park. Just outside the Zoödóhos Piyí Monastery at Aryínia is the only spring on Mt. Énos, where the wild horses in the park come to drink. The mountain and the whole area around it produce excellent honey, which you can often find for sale in private houses: look for a sign with the words ΘΥΜΑΡΙΣΙΟ ΜΕΛΙ ('Thyme honey').

Continuing from Markópoulo, you come soon to **Pástra**, the administrative centre of the Municipality of Eliós-Prónni. Here, as at Platiés, there is a cheese-dairy where you can sample and buy local cheeses. At the side of the town hall there is a concrete-surfaced side road leading downhill. Follow this and it turns into a path that runs by the side of the stream and brings you

Roasting corn on the cob in the village square at Skála.

One of 'Our Lady's snakes' on the arm of a Dutch tourist.

103

Póros.

out at Káto Kateliós: look out for the wooden signposts and yellow way-marks. Along the way you will pass several ruined water-mills that used to grind flour for the villages round about.

Ancient Pronnoi, one of the four cities of the Kephallenian tetrapolis, stood on the hill above Pástra. Still standing on the summit of the hill, now called **Paliókastro** ('Old Castle'), are some impressive remains of the fortification walls of the Classical acropolis (citadel). In popular usage the acropolis is known as Kástro tis Syriás, a corruption of Kástro tis Oriás ('Castle of the Beautiful Maiden').

At **Áyios Yeóryios**, the next village, there are two side roads branching

10

The village square at Tzannáta with its lofty plane trees and unfailing spring.

105

Enjoying the evening view at Póros.

off from the main road to Póros: (a) a turning to the left by the side of the church leads to the mountain villages of **Xenópoulo**, **Kapandríti**, **Andreoláta** and **Kambitsáta**, on the south-eastern slopes of Mt. Énos; (b) a minor road off to the right, which soon degenerates into a dirt road, leads to the old villages of the mountainous region between Póros and Skála, now almost uninhabited: **Asproyérakas**, **Annináta**, **Spathí**, **Faniés** and **Koutroukói**. Since 1953 most of the inhabitants have moved down to the villages on the coast.

The sharp bends in the road after Áyios Yeóryios give you a good view of the terraces built so laboriously to make strips of flat, cultivable land on the mountainsides and prevent the soil from being washed away. The road to Póros goes through **Ayía Iríni**, a village surrounded by orchards in the mountain-encircled plain of Arákli, with rushing streams and rich natural vegetation. From there it goes on to **Tzannáta**, where there is a fine Mycenaean tholos tomb.

From Tzannáta a turning off to the left leads to Sámi. The main road bends eastwards and runs through a gorge to **Póros**. The Póros gorge is one of the most stunning geological formations on Kefaloniá. Both sides are almost vertical cliffs, 80 metres high, and in winter and spring the River Vóhinas tumbles noisily along the stream bed between them, with plane trees growing on its banks, before flowing into the sea at Póros.

In the Póros gorge is the Drákena Cave, which was inhabited from earliest antiquity.

106

A book exhibition in the square at Póros.

The Mycenaean tomb at Tzannáta (1350 B.C.).

The tomb at Boúrdzi, just outside Tzannáta, in a lovely setting of olive trees, cypresses and oaks, was discovered in 1991 and excavated by the archaeologist Dr. Lázaros Kolónas. It is the biggest tholos tomb yet found in north-western Greece: the chamber has a diameter of 6.80 m. and the walls of the vault are standing to a height of 3.95 m. The roof of the vault fell in, probably during the Venetian period, and the tomb remained buried under the hill until its recent rediscovery. It had been looted in antiquity but still contained some valuable grave goods. Some of the finds, including clay vases, gold jewellery, sealstones, a miniature gold axe, two gold rosettes,

The entrance to the Mycenaean tomb at Tzannáta.

a gold plaquette with a relief of a paper nautilus, gold beads and plaquettes of glass paste, can be seen in the Argostóli Archaeological Museum.

The size of the tomb, the nature of the burial offerings found there and its well-chosen position point to the existence of an important Mycenaean town in the vicinity. This may perhaps be significant in connection with the ongoing excavations in search of the capital of Homer's Ithaka.

Opening hours: Tuesday-Sunday 08:30-15:00. Closed on Mondays and public holidays.

Interesting finds brought to light in recent excavations – tools made of stone and bone, figurines, pottery and so on – tell us a good deal about the use of the cave in prehistoric and historic times. Finds from the Classical period indicate that the cave was then associated with the cult of the Nymphs. The name Drákena ('She-Dragon') refers to the local legend of a dragon that lived in the gorge: in the popular imagination, certain marks in the rocks on the sides of the gorge were believed to be the dragon's footprints.

The whole area around Póros bears witness to a historical continuity going back thousands of years. The Classical acropolis on the hill now called Paliókastro, 3 km. inland and 545 m. above sea level, the ancient acropolis on Mt. Pakhní overlooking modern Póros, the Drákena Cave on the south side of the gorge and the Mycenaean royal tholos tomb at Tzannáta have aroused great interest among archaeologists.

The village of Póros stretches along the beautiful seashore. Its attractive combination of sea and mountain and the good fishing to be had in its waters won it a loyal following of regular visitors from the earliest years of tourist development on the island. Nearby beaches are **Ráyia**, **Liménia** and **Makriá Pétra** (the last of these is only accessible by boat). Because the village is so long, the main square in the middle plays an important part in local social life. Youngsters play games while their elders stroll about or sit in animated conversation until late in the evening. The one bank is also in the middle of the village. Theatrical and musical performances and other events are held in summer in the main square and also in the semicircular open-air theatre, the only one of its kind on the island. A sporting event that has become an established tradition in recent years is the Telemacheios (Tilemáhios) cross-country race along the coast road from Skála to Póros, held every year in early September.

109

Makriá Pétra beach.

110

Drawing water from the well at the Monastery of the Theotókos Átrou.

The modern port of Póros, which in antiquity was the port of Pronnoi, is used by fishing boats, water buses and pleasure boats, and there is a regular ferry service to Póros from Killíni on the mainland. Blocks of stone from the ancient harbour works are still clearly visible on the seabed.

Two kilometres out of Póros on the way back to Argostóli, 500 m. after the road emerges from the gorge, a minor road branches off to the right and climbs up through oak woods to the oldest religious house on the island, the ninth-century **Monastery of the Theotókos Átrou** (the Virgin of Átros). It stands at an altitude of 500 m. in a remote spot near the summit of Mt. Átros. The iconostasis in the small, newly-built church is the original one from the church destroyed by the 1953 earthquakes. The medieval tower next to the church contains the monastery's old wine press, where the grapes were trodden with the feet in the traditional way. The old monastic cells can still be seen. The monastery's water supply came from wells in the precinct. A short distance to the west of the monastery there is a beautiful plateau where the olive trees grow to a great size: here the monks had their vineyard. The monastery commands a panoramic of the sea and the nearby islands, and in the evening you can see Zákinthos glowing golden in the sunset.

111

The Monastery of the Theotókos Átrou.

Walks: • **In the plain of Eliós: Kateliós - Hionáta - Thirámona - Mavráta - Kateliós.** Near Thirámona is the lovely, little-frequented beach of Koróni; the last stretch of the path down to the sea is very steep. Time: 4 hrs.

• **Skála - Póros along the coast road.** On the way you pass numerous small beaches and coves: care is needed on the paths down to them. At Liménia, just before the road climbs over the hill to Póros, there is a long beach. Take water with you. Time: 3 hrs. (Return to Skála by bus).

• **Póros - the gorge - Mycenaean royal tholos tomb at Tzannáta - Póros.** Look out for the signpost to the Mycenaean tomb as you enter Tzannáta. Quench your thirst with delicious mountain water from the never-failing spring under the plane trees in the village square of Tzannáta. Time: 1½ hrs.

• **Póros - the gorge - Átros Monastery - Póros.** Five hundred metres after the end of the gorge turn right and follow the road to the monastery (clearly signposted). Take water with you. Time: 3 hrs. Since the abbot is usually away on Sundays, it is best to do this walk on a weekday if you want to find the monastery open.

Useful phone numbers

Skála
• Police Station 2671 083 100
• Fire Brigade 199
• Doctor's Surgery 2671 083 222
• Taxis 2671 083 231

Hionáta
• Post Office 2671 081 238

Pástra
• Eliós-Prónni Municipal Offices 2671 081 701

Póros
• Police Station 2674 072 210
• Port Police 2674 072 460
• Doctor's Surgery 2674 072 552
• Taxis 2674 072 909 / 2674 072 230
• Bus Station 2674 022 024

For tourist information

• G.N.T.O. 2671 022 248
• Póros Municipal Information Office 2674 072 000
• Póros Police Station 2674 072 210
• Skála Municipal Information Office 2671 083 201
• Skála Police Station 2671 083 100

1

'The Great Mountain from Eliós'. Watercolour by Diána Andonakátou.

Póros - Piryí district - Sámi

Retrace your steps from Póros as far as Tzannáta, and there take the right turn to Sámi. The first village you come to is **Áyios Nikólaos**, nestling amid the greenery of the forest-clad mountains. The hillsides round about, where the air is laden with the scent of aromatic herbs (oregano, thyme, mint, sage, fennel), offer a home to partridges, woodcock and many other species of birds. A signpost on the road marks the beginning of the footpath to **Lake Ávithos**, better known locally as Lake Ákoli. Lakes, even small ones, are few and far between on the islands. Lake Ákoli, which has water all the year round and is about 10 m. deep, is fed from the aquifers of Mt. Énos and was formerly believed to be bottomless (which is the meaning of both its names in Greek). The lake is the source of the River Vóhinas, which irrigates the whole area. In the past there were several water-powered flour-mills along its banks, and the same is true of other rivers in the Eliós district. Beyond Áyios Nikólaos the road continues through the mountain villages of **Harákti**, **Digalétto** and **Tsakarissiáno**, all about 500 m. above sea level.

In this rugged, forested country there are a lot of ruined forts and towers, some dating from antiquity and some from later periods. They were built to control the area, which was important because it lay between the two ancient

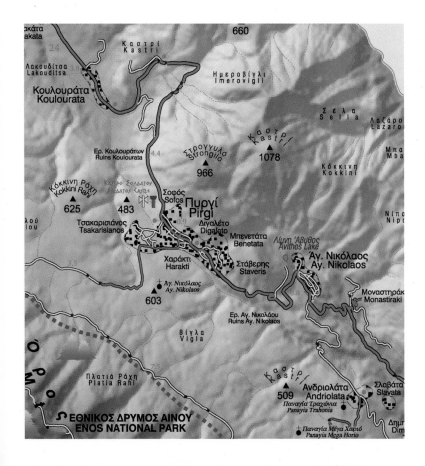

113

Ruins of an ancient building in Soldáto Castle.

ports of Same and Pronnoi, and to protect the valuable timber of the Énos forests. One such fort was Soldáto Castle: near the ruins of the castle you will see some trimly-dressed semicircular blocks of stone, which probably came from an altar of Zeus.

To drive up Mt. Énos from the Piryí district, turn left at Harákti. After about 10 km. you come to the chapel of Áyios Elefthérios, where you turn left for the summit.

Further along the road to Sámi are the villages of **Koulouráta**, **Zerváta** and **Grizáta**. At Koulouráta there is a riding school that arranges horseback treks on Mt. Énos. After **Tzanetáta** you join the main road from Argostóli to Sámi: turn right for Sámi (see below).

11.

Lake Ávithos.

Argostóli - Drongaráti Cave - Sámi - Melissáni Cave - Ayía Efimía

To go to Sámi from Argostóli, you can either cross the Drápanos bridge or start out on the Póros road and take the first turning to the left, driving right round the Koútavos lagoon until you rejoin the Drápanos bridge road. You then follow the signposts to Sámi. Almost immediately you cross a small bridge beneath which is the chapel of Ayía Varvára, hewn out of the rock.

The first turning off the Sámi road is to the left, to the attractive villages of **Farakláta** and **Dilináta**. Robóla grapes are grown in the vineyards round about, on the foothills of the mountain.

The Church of the Evangelístria in the middle of Farakláta has the tallest

Andíssamos beach.

campanile on the island. The national poet of Romania, Panait Istrati (1884-1935), was the son of an immigrant who came from Farakláta: his real name was Yerásimos Valsamís.

Dilináta is a big village lying at an altitude of 400 m. on the west slope of Mt. Evmorfía. Most of the villagers make their living from sheep and goats and the village produces large quantities of cheese and other dairy products. From there an old mulepath runs north through the rugged mountains to the Pílaros district (see p.108).

Continuing along the main road to Sámi, shortly before **Razáta** you come

11

Part of the acropolis wall of Krane.

to a turning off to the right which leads to the ruined Cyclopean walls of the great **acropolis of ancient Krane** (6th cent. B.C.). The way into the archaeological site is signposted and is an easy walk. It is worth seeing how the ancient Greeks built large fortification walls out of these huge, trimmed stones: even today, when we have advanced technology at our disposal, it would be a remarkable feat. Also visible in the site are the ruins of a Doric temple dedicated to Demeter, the goddess of agriculture in general and cereals in particular. The area around ancient Krane is farming country,

117

The road from Argostóli to Sámi.

planted mainly with vines and olive trees. Opposite the church at Razáta is the Lavrángas Park, a large expanse of pine-woods. This was the home of Dioníssis Lavrángas (1864-1941), a well-known composer and founder of the Hellenic Opera, for the last years of his life. Lavrángas studied in Paris and Milan and was for a time the choirmaster of the Argostóli Philharmonic School before moving to Athens, where he taught at the Athens Conservatoire.

Ten minutes' drive beyond the turning to ancient Krane you enter the Commune of Omalá (see p. 139), where the Convent of Áyios Yerásimos (St. Gerásimos, the island's patron saint) is situated. This is the heart of Robóla country, where the best-known Kefalonian wine

118

A concert in the Drongaráti Cave.

is produced. From there the main road climbs over Mt. Énos (see p. 142), which has the highest peak in the Ionian Islands, before snaking down through thick vegetation to Sámi – the ancient Same, which was one of the four city-states of the Kephallenian tetrapolis. The earliest mention of Same occurs in Homer.

The whole of this region is full of caves. In fact Greece has more caves in relation to its size than any other country: so far about 7,500 have been recorded. Of the few that have been opened up for tourism, two are in the Sámi district: the Drongaráti Cave and the lake cave of Melissáni.

A few kilometres before Sámi there is a turning off to the left to **Haliotáta**, the nearest village to the **Drongaráti Cave.** The cave consists of two chambers. In the first one the roof has fallen in. A sloping corridor 44 m. long leads down to a level-floored semicircular chamber measuring approximately 65x45 m. and about 20 m. high, full of wonderful stalactites. Because of its excellent acoustics it is known as the Chamber of the Apotheosis, and concerts are sometimes held here. In summer the cave is open to visitors daily, 9:00-19:00.

In the next village, **Pouláta**, is the privately-owned Church of Áyios Spirídon, built in the eighteenth century, when Kefaloniá had a total of 350-400 private, public and parish churches. This particular church, situated right at the top of the village towards the mountain, is a scheduled historic monument, and its wood-carvings – on the throne and the iconostasis and in the women's gallery – are exquisitely done and of considerable artistic merit. At the time of writing, restoration work is still in progress. On the floor of the church there is a relief of a two-headed eagle, the emblem of the Byzantine Empire that is to be seen in nearly all Greek Orthodox churches, either over a doorway or on the floor. Its presence in the church indicates the adherence of clergy and laity alike to the Orthodox faith, and it symbolizes the sense of Greek national identity felt by the Ionian Islanders, who were subjected to Catholic propaganda. To visit the church, ask for the key at the house next door.

119

The two-headed eagle in the Church of Áyios Spirídon at Pouláta.

Besides the Drongaráti and Melissáni caves, there are other caves and potholes in the Sámi area that have not been commercially developed. Near Pouláta is the Angaláki Cave, hidden among the trees and shrubs. The mouth of the cave is a huge hole measuring 40x30 m, from which a vertical chimney descends for 30 m. At the bottom there is a heap of rocks about 10 m. high, where the roof of the cave fell in. Leading away from the base of the heap are two sloping galleries, each with a forest of stalactites, running down to an underground lake. North of the Angaláki Cave is the Áyii Theódori Hole, which measures 22x12 m. at its mouth and is 55 m. deep, with a lake (28x13 m.) at the bottom. Further west is the Ayía Eleoússa Hole, also surrounded by dense vegetation, which measures 23x20 m. at its mouth and has a vertical depth of 65 m. Near Karavómilos is the Zerváti Hole, 18 m. deep, with freshwater lakes at the bottom. Also in the Sámi district is the Hiridóni Cave, where a vertical 40 m. descent leads down to a chamber 100 m. long, again with water at the far end.

Sámi, a small seaside town on the gulf of the same name, stands on the site of the port of ancient Same, with Itháki visible just across the water. The modern harbour is in roughly the same position as the ancient one: it is the busiest port on Kefaloniá, with regular ferries plying to the other Ionian Islands, mainland Greece and Italy. The bustle of arrivals and departures lends the town an air of cheerful liveliness. The waterfront is lined with tavernas and cafés facing the moored fishing boats and yachts. In the

120

Fishermen in Sámi harbour (early 19th cent.).

The port of **Sámi** has been used by the ships of many nations, some of them arriving with hostile intent, others for trade. In the early years of the second century B.C. the Romans, needing bases from which to launch military operations against Greece, set their sights on the Ionian Islands. After Kerkyra (Corfu) it was the turn of Zakynthos and Kephallenia. Kephallenia was particularly important for two reasons: the forests on Mt. Ainos provided a valuable source of timber for shipbuilding, and something had to be done about the pirates who lurked on the island and were constantly attacking Roman merchant ships on their way past. In 189 B.C. three of

121

the four Kephallenian city-states submitted to Rome, but the people of Same put up a heroic resistance from their acropolis, which they called **Kyatis**. The blockade lasted for four months, and the Romans had to bring in reinforcements before they eventually (in 188 B.C.) succeeded in overcoming the Samians. The city was then sacked, the surviving inhabitants were sold as slaves and Same became an important Roman naval base.

The hills of Áyii Fanéndes and Paliókastro, overlooking the modern town, have extensive ruins of the walls of the ancient acropolis called Kyatis, built of smoothly-dressed rectangular blocks of stone. The walls had a total distance of 3.5 km., enclosing the summits of both hills. Near the foot of **Áyii Fanéndes hill** there is a spot popularly called Rakóspito (probably a corruption of Drakóspito, 'Dragon House'), where there are some remains of a Roman building. A mosaic floor was found nearby, as well as a fine Roman bronze head which is now in the Argostóli Archaeological Museum. On Áyii Fanéndes hill (alt. 270 m.) are the ruins of the monastery of the same name, founded in the thirteenth century and finally abandoned in the nineteenth. The ruined chapel of Áyios Nikólaos close by has some magnificent frescoes.

One of the gates of the ancient acropolis of Same, in a painting done about 170 years ago by Charles Napier, the British Resident.

122

12

View of Sámi.

evenings that stretch of road is closed to traffic, and people congregate there to meet their friends and relax. The town has a busy shopping centre with a post office and several banks. A summer festival is held at Sámi every year, with performances and events of various kinds for all ages.

In the Church of the Theotókos in the middle of the town you will see an icon of the Panayía Glikofiloússa (the Virgin of Tenderness). She is the patroness of Sámi and the icon is one of the most important treasures of ecclesiastical art on the island. The icon, dated 1736 but unsigned, shows the stylistic influence of Renaissance art in Western Europe and is probably by Stéfanos Tzangarólas or one of his pupils. The inscription at the top left (Η ΜΟΝΗ ΕΛΠΙΣ ΤΩΝ ΑΠΕΛΠΙΣΜΕΝΩΝ) means 'Sole hope of those who despair'. Tradition has it that the Venetian admiral Sebastian Venier dedicated this icon to the Monastery of Áyii Fanéndes near Sámi after the great victory of the combined European Christian fleet over the Turks at Lepanto (Náfpaktos) in 1571.

124

The icon of the Panayía Glikofiloússa (the Virgin of Tenderness).

A minor road running north-east along the coast from the little square near the harbour leads past the ruins of the ancient acropolis and the ruined Monastery of Áyii Fanéndes to the Monastery of the Panayía Agrilíon, which has a medieval bell-tower and commands a fine view over the Ionian Sea, the Gulf of Sámi, Itháki and the lovely beach of Andíssamos.

From the Panayía Agrilíon the road runs down to **Andíssamos**, a long, horseshoe-shaped beach in a natural amphitheatre of tree-clad slopes. Andíssamos beach was one of the locations used for the film *Captain Corelli's Mandolin*, a major production based on the novel by Louis de Bernières, which was shot in the Sámi area in 2000.

The road leading west out of Sámi and then turning north-west goes to the Pílaros district. On the way it takes you through the village of **Karavómilos** and past the **Melissáni Cave.**

At Karavómilos the road bends to the right, towards the seashore. Here there is a pretty little lake where much of the water that disappears into the *katavóthres* or swallow-holes at Argostóli (see p. 56) reappears on the surface. On its long underground journey the seawater from the *katavóthres*

125

The medieval bell-tower of the Monastery of the Panayía Agrilíon.

126

North of Sámi, near Karavómilos, is the **lake cave of Melissáni**, 500 m. inland from the sea. Since part of the roof has collapsed, the water in the lake is constantly changing colour under the dancing sunbeams. The iridescence of the water is reflected on to the stalactites and the cave walls, creating a magical kaleidoscopic effect. The hole in the roof measures 50x40 m. and the water level is about 25 m. below the roof. The lake is 163 m. long, 25 m. wide and between 10 and 30 m. deep. In the 1960s a tunnel was made through the rock for easier access to the cave. You will be taken round the lake in a small boat, going first to the part that is open to the sky and then into the dark. Just before you leave the daylight you will see a small islet formed by the rocks falling in from the roof. The water from Melissáni flows into the Karavómilos lake.

127

In 1951, when the cave was first explored, an ancient lamp was found on the islet; and in 1963, under Spyros Marinátos, archaeologists found a clay figurine of Pan, a disc with a relief of Pan surrounded by dancing nymphs and a sherd with a relief of a female figure, all on the islet. In a recent book on Homeric Ithaka, arguing that Homeric Ithaka was in fact Kephallenia, Melissáni is identified as the 'Cave of the Nymphs' described in the *Odyssey*.

In summer the cave is open daily, 08:00-18:00.

Inside the Melissáni lake cave.

129

Karavómilos.

130

mixes with fresh ground water, so the water in the lake is brackish. If you walk along the shore hereabouts you will see a lot of underground streams flowing into the sea: they are all part of the same phenomenon. The lakeside, with its shade trees, children's playground and taverna, is a pleasant place to rest from the rigours of sightseeing. Karavómilos (formerly called Vlaháta) takes its name from the mill (*mílos*) that once stood on the shore: the millwheel (actually a paddle-wheel from an old steamer) was turned by the flow of water from the underground stream.

The main road continues northwestwards, running close to the beautiful rocky coast with small coves here and there. At **Ayía Paraskeví beach** there are watersports facilities. The next place you come to is Ayía Efimía, in the Pílaros district.

Walks: • **Sámi - ancient acropolis of Kyatis - Áyii Fanéndes - chapel of Áyios Yeóryios - Sámi.** The road leading east from the little square at the far end of the harbour starts off uphill but stays close to the coast. Follow the signs for Áyii Fanéndes. Take water with you. Time 2½ hrs.

• **Sámi - Monastery of the Panayía Agrilíon - Andíssamos beach - Sámi.** Start along the road to Áyii Fanéndes but follow the signs to Moní Agrilíon. For Andíssamos beach continue along the road on which you started out. Refreshments can be obtained at Andíssamos. Time: 3 hrs.

• **Sámi - Pouláta - Drongaráti Cave - Sámi.** Start out along the road to Karavómilos and Melissáni. Soon after the Sámi camping site (on your right) the Pouláta road branches off to the left. Go through Pouláta and on to Haliotáta, and after Haliotáta turn right for the Drongaráti Cave. From there it is 5 km. back to Sámi. Time: 3 hrs.

• **Sámi - Karavómilos - Melissáni - Sámi.** Along the road, following the signposts. Time: 1½ hrs.

• The area around Sámi is good cycling country.

Useful phone numbers

Sámi
- Police Station 2674 022 100
- Fire Brigade 199
- Port Police 2674 022 031
- Health Centre 2674 022 222 / 2674 022 807
- Town Hall 2674 022 019
- Post Office 2674 022 012
- Taxis 2674 022 308 / 2674 022 808

For tourist information
- G.N.T.O. 2671 022 248
- Sámi Town Hall 2674 022 019
- Sámi Police Station 2674 022 100

The church door in the Monastery of the Panayía Agrilíon.

Ayía Efimía - Mírtos - Ássos - Fiskárdo

Ayía Efimía, an attractive village which is the centre of the **Pílaros** district, lies 9 km. north-west of Sámi. The district was named Pílaros (from *píli*, gate) because in antiquity the harbour of Ayía Efimía was the main gateway to the northern part of the island. The village is named after the Church of Ayía Efimía, while the little white chapel on the quayside is dedicated to St. Nicholas (Áyios Nikólaos). Ayía Efimía is popular with yachtsmen: in summer the harbour is full of pleasure boats and the mixture of languages coming out of the tavernas and bars gives the place quite a cosmopolitan air. The pedestrianized road running northwards from the centre along the beautiful seashore, where striated rocks alternate with little sandy beaches, is a good place for a relaxing stroll in the evening. Sámi and Itháki are clearly visible across the sea. Boats and canoes can be hired on the waterfront in the centre of the village and there is a diving school for those who want to explore the delights of the seabed. A few grand houses still standing around the bay testify to the importance that Ayía Efimía enjoyed in former times,

View of Ayía Efimía   132

133

Boating in Ayía Efimía harbour, 1951.

134

Pear trees by the seashore near Ayía Efimía.

when it was the commercial centre of the whole region and small coasters laden with cargo, passengers, mail and newspapers plied regularly to and from Sámi, Itháki and Fiskárdo. The ruins of a Roman villa with fine mosaics and ornamentation, water pipes and drainage and heating systems has been discovered not far from Ayía Efimía. Ask for directions in the village.

At Ayía Efimía you have a choice of three roads to continue exploring northern Kefaloniá: **1.** A minor road to the left, before the centre of the village, leads to the mountain villages at the foot of Mt. Ayía Dinatí. After **Drakáta**, follow the signposts for Mírtos, Ássos and Fiskárdo (all in the Érissos peninsula). **2.** The main road to the left from the middle of the village and out through the plain of Ayía Efimía takes you directly to Mírtos and the rest of the Érissos peninsula. **3.** The road to the north, near the east coast, takes you to Neohóri, Komitáta, Vassilikádes and Fiskárdo.

A. Route **1.** Inland from Ayía Efimía is a fertile plain bounded on the south by Mt. Ayía Dinatí (1,131 m.) and on the north by Mt. Kalón Óros (901 m.). In the picturesque villages of **Drakopouláta**, **Vassilopouláta** and **Makrióttika**, at the foot of Mt. Ayía Dinatí, many aspects of life have changed little over the years. The best way to see them is on foot. Most of the houses have gardens with almond and pomegranate trees as well as flowers. In this area you will come across some small churches that survived the 1953 earth-

13

A house at Drakopouláta.

quakes, and also derelict windmills and water-mills that have long been defunct. Makriótika has a picturesque village square with a panoramic view of the surrounding country. The biggest institution there is the district Dairy Co-operative, renowned for its excellent cheeses – especially feta – and other products. Cheese-makers from the Pílaros district were known far and wide: not only in the rest of Greece but elsewhere in the Balkans and in southern Italy too. Large flocks of sheep and goats are to be seen grazing on the mountains round about and the sound of their bells is heard everywhere. Stylianós Moschópoulos, a former grazier, has written an article in which he explains the purpose of the bells. One reason is that the greediest animals (and there are some of those in every flock) tend to wander away from the rest in search of good grazing, and the shepherd puts bells round their necks so that he can hear where they are. Secondly, in the heat of summer the bells of the grazing animals encourage the lazier ones to graze too. Last but not least, the gentle clonking of the bells, all on different notes and with different tones, makes a very pleasant musical sound.

Strange though it may seem, the sheep and goats that graze on Mt. Ayía Dinatí have shiny golden teeth! This curious phenomenon is caused by the elements in the soil. The first person to refer to goats with 'gold teeth' on Kefaloniá was Aristotle in the fifth century B.C. Another odd tradition mentioned in ancient literature is that the goats on the mountains of Kefaloniá do

Cheese is an important item in the Greek diet, so much so that the per capita consumption of cheese in Greece is the highest in Europe. The Greeks eat cheese morning, noon and night, either on its own or with other food, and forty per cent of the cheese consumed is feta. Kefaloniá is renowned for the quality of its feta. The sheep and goats range freely on the mountains where there is a wide variety of grasses, trees, shrubs and aromatic herbs that give a distinctive taste to the milk and the cheese made from it. It is

136

estimated that there are 150,000 sheep and goats on Kefaloniá, which is equivalent to four animals for every man, woman and child on the island!

Feta is still made in the traditional way. The taste depends on the salt content, the temperature at which enzymes are added and the way the cheese is strained. Most feta is made of a mixture of sheep's milk (about 70%) and goat's milk (about 30%). Other types of cheese made on Kefaloniá include mizíthra, kefalotíri and graviéra.

137

Goats near Mírtos.

138

An old stone hut in the Érissos district.

not drink water in winter: when they are thirsty, they just open their mouths. There may be some truth in this story, because the mountain air is so damp in winter, what with the cold weather and low clouds, that the goats can perhaps get enough moisture simply by breathing it in.

Above Makriótika, in a superb position amid the holly-oaks and pine trees, is the seventeenth-century Monastery of the Most Holy Virgin better known as the Themáton Monastery or Monastery of the Thémata. The icon of the Panayía Anatolikoú in the monastery is said to have miraculous powers, and people pray to the Virgin as represented in this icon to resolve the problems (*thémata*) bothering them. The monastery used to have a very good library containing sumptuous gilt-bound editions of works by Voltaire, Rousseau and others: these books are said to have been given to the monastery by French republican officials in exchange for old manuscripts which they took away with them. From the monastery there is a breathtaking view over the mountains and across the sea to Itháki and the coast of Akarnanía.

B. **Route 2.** Branching off from the main road across the plain of Ayía Efimía there are minor roads to the villages on Mt. Kalón Óros, including **Dendrináta**, **Andipáta** and **Karoussáta**. Dendrináta was the birthplace of Marínos Antípas (1872-1907), a pioneering socialist who was a leading figure in the farm workers' protest movement at a time when those who worked on the land in Greece were hostages to the big landowners. Antípas was assassinated in Thessaly for his 'subversive' activities. He is commemorated by a statue by the side of the main road in Potamianáta. At Divaráta, turn right for Mírtos, Ássos and Fiskárdo.

139

Statue of Marínos Antípas, the militant socialist, at Potamianáta.

C. Route 3. The road running north near the east coast takes you through Neohóri, Komitáta and Vassilikádes to Fiskárdo, running parallel with the east coast at an altitude of about 400 m. **Neohóri** and **Komitáta** are small villages built on hilltops as a precaution against the pirate raids of past centuries. Hereabouts the terrain is rockier and there is not nearly as much vegetation as in the southern part of the island. Everywhere the hillsides are terraced to provide a bit of level, cultivable land for growing vegetables and grapevines. Beside most of the houses and in the fields you will see cisterns built to collect the rainwater. Keep an eye open for the round stone huts in the fields, which survived the 1953 earthquakes: they were used for storage and as resting-places for the farmers when they were on their land. For the route from Vassilikádes to Fiskárdo see below.

From **Divaráta** a road snakes steeply down to the stunning beach of **Mírtos**, one of the most glittering gems in Kefaloniá's crown. Users of the website *www.thalassa.gr* have voted it the best beach in Greece, and some rate it the best in Europe. In fact it has even been named as one of the three best in the world! The glittering white beach and limpid turquoise waters, set against a backdrop of precipitous cliffs and awe-inspiring mountainsides,

140

Mírtos beach.

create a sublime image that is not easily forgotten. It is worth staying here until the early evening to see the sunset. People driving along the main road to Fiskárdo often stop to admire the view from above. Every August holidaymakers flock to Mírtos from all over the island for the concert that is given on the beach at full moon.

The shortest route from Argostóli to the north of the island (Mírtos, Ássos and Fiskárdo) is to start out along the Lixoúri road through the Thiniá district and keep straight on at Kardakáta.

After Mírtos you enter the Érissos district, the northernmost part of Kefaloniá. Thanks to its outstanding natural beauty and traditional-style villages (many of which survived the earthquakes virtually unharmed), **Érissos** is a 'must' for most visitors to the island.

141

Windmills in the Pílaros district, 1930.

Ássos, a village at the near end of a narrow isthmus, can be seen from afar. The isthmus, flanked by two lovely little bays, leads to a peninsula rising to 155 m. above sea level, crowned by a fortress built by the Venetians. In the village are a number of grand houses which, though in a poor state of preservation, indicate its importance in the Venetian period. Ássos is one of the most attractive villages in Kefaloniá: it still retains its authentic character and has few souvenir shops. The tavernas, shaded by plane trees, are right next to the sheltered harbour where the fishing boats lie at their moorings. There is a beach for swimmers, and in summer yachts come in large numbers to anchor in the bays on both sides of the isthmus.

After Ássos the road veers away from the coast and runs through the middle of the Érissos peninsula. Along the way there are side roads leading through beautiful countryside, where the typical garigue vegetation of Spanish broom and kermes oaks is interspersed with olive-groves and punctuated with clumps of cypresses, to little villages that are pretty as pictures, dotted about the green mountainsides: **Kothréas**, with a magnificent view of Ássos, **Vassilikádes**, the centre of the Érissos district, **Mesovoúnia**, **Konidaráta** and **Mánganos** are some of them. In the area between **Defaranáta**, **Patrikáta**, **Kariá** and **Varí**, in verdant country full of large kermes oaks, is Paliohérsou Monastery, founded before 1600. The locality of the monastery is called Perivóli ('Garden' or 'Orchard'), because it was once full of vineyards growing currant vines. To visit the monastery, stop at Defaranáta and ask for information. Near the village of **Playiá** there is a small Classical acropolis, well hidden by the dense vegetation, on a hilltop commanding a superb view of the surrounding country and Itháki.

Before you reach Fiskárdo you pass two fine beaches. At **Tzamareláta**

142

Ássos.

there is a turning off to the left signposted to the little bay of **Ayía Ierousalím**, and just one kilometre before Fiskárdo there is a signpost to **Émblisi** beach (Paralía Émplysi), where you can swim in the crystal-clear turquoise sea and enjoy one of the loveliest views in Kefaloniá, looking towards Lefkáda, the offshore islets and the high mountains of Aitolo-Akarnanía.

The road from Mánganos to Fiskárdo runs through the most northerly villages in Kefaloniá, **Andipáta** and **Yermanáta**. At Mánganos there is a turning to the right that takes you along a minor road to Fiskárdo through **Tselendáta** and **Matsoukáta**, finally following the coastline past pretty coves and seaside hamlets. Some of the beaches, such as **Fóki**, have olive-groves stretching almost down to the water's edge, offering shade from the summer sun.

Fiskárdo, a picturesque village undamaged by the 1953 earthquakes, where old-style Kefalonian houses are still the order of the day, is a sched-

143

The main gate of the fortress at Ássos.

The history of the **Ássos fortress** dates back to 1574, when the Council of Kefaloniá sent a delegation to Venice to petition for a new castle to protect the island against attack by Turks and pirates. The one existing castle, that of St. George near Argostóli, was inadequate to keep the island's shores safe, and the Ássos peninsula was chosen as the site of the new fortress, because its sheer cliffs and precipitous slopes provided natural fortifications that made it virtually impregnable. Construction started in 1593 and the fortress was completed in the remarkably short time of two years, as we are informed by the Latin inscription built into the wall above the main gate. Work continued throughout the first half of the seventeenth century and a great deal of money was spent on it. The walls, enclosing an irregular rectangle with a perimeter of three kilometres, were reinforced with five bastions at the highest points. The main gatehouse was on the east side, with a vaulted corridor; there was also a postern gate on the south side and a smaller postern leading out to the north-west corner of the peninsula. Most of the public buildings, including the garrison headquarters, the Provveditore's residence and the Catholic Church of St. Mark, were located just inside the main gate: they are now so ruined as to be hardly recognizable. In 1685, according to the Venetian geographer Vicenzo Coronelli, there were sixty public and two hundred private buildings in the enceinte. Ássos lost some of its strategic importance in 1684, when the Venetians recaptured Lefkáda (Santa Maura) from the Turks. Its harbour had never been of much value to the Venetian fleet, not only because of its small size (it could only take 5-10 galleys) but also because it continually needed dredging.

In the first period of French rule (1797-1799) Ássos was the administrative centre of a temporary municipality. In 1930

Ássos in an eighteenth-century print.   144

an agricultural prison was established inside the fortress, but it was closed after the 1953 earthquakes. The fortress is now covered by the 'Kastron Periplous' programme and work has started on its improvement and development.

145

Old Venetian houses at Ássos.

uled 'traditional settlement' subject to stringent restrictions on the demolition and alteration of buildings, and the whole area round about is one of outstanding natural beauty. The name Fiskárdo is a corruption of Guiscard: Robert Guiscard, a Norman adventurer who conquered northern Kefaloniá,

146

Tselendáta, with a view of Itháki and Lefkáda.

147

An alleyway in Fiskárdo.

died at Panormos in 1085. (Panormos was the village's old name: it means 'well-protected bay'.) Fiskárdo is the northernmost harbour in Kefaloniá and has become one of the most popular ports of call for yachtsmen in the Ionian Sea. With its forests, its less forbidding hills and mountains and its deserted coves, it is an ideal centre for quiet holidays 'far from the madding crowd'.

No motor vehicles are allowed in old Fiskárdo: cars have to be left in the car park at the entrance to the village. When you walk through the narrow streets and alleys, looking at the well-preserved old houses, you will have no difficulty in understanding why it is considered the most beautiful village on the island. Although there are a number of tavernas and bars, there are few

148

View of Fiskárdo.

shops, only one bank and a post office. Ample accommodation is available in hotels, holiday apartments and private houses in the area, and some old houses have been restored, renovated and turned into guesthouses. Small ferries run from here to Lefkáda and Itháki. In summer the harbour is crammed full of yachts, and boats can be rented at the small jetty. In winter Fiskárdo presents a very different picture: like most seaside villages in Greece, it then reverts to being a quiet community with a small population and a few fishing boats at their moorings along the quayside.

The old primary school is now the home of the Fiskárdo Nautical and Environmental Club. One of the classrooms is used as a museum containing posters and other visual aids with information about the natural and marine environment. One of the most interesting sections of the exhibition is the one on the Mediterranean monk seal, an endangered species sometimes found off unfrequented rocky shores in Kefaloniá and the seas round about.

The area around Fiskárdo is of considerable archaeological interest. Palaeolithic stone tools have been found on the **Fourniá** peninsula. In historical times Fiskárdo was a town of some importance, owing to its geographical position and its safe harbour. The peak of its prosperity is attested by the imposing ruins of an Early Christian basilica and two towers of the sixth century A.D. at Palátia on the Fourniá peninsula. The towers are standing to a height of 6 m. Most probably there had been a temple of Apollo on this site, as in other places on the island: Apollo was the god of the sun, patron of seafarers and guardian of harbours. A Roman cemetery has recently been excavated near the shore to the east of the centre of the village.

At Andipáta, Halikerí, Tzamareláta and Varí, in northern Érissos, you will see some fine churches both old (i.e. pre-1953) and new, with interesting wall-paintings.

149

The Early Christian basilica at Fiskárdo.

The Mediterranean monk seal (**Mona-chus monachus**) is the biggest mammal found in Greece and has inhabited Greek waters since antiquity. It is mentioned by Homer: Menelaos disguised himself in a sealskin to visit Proteus, the 'Old Man of the Sea', to find out how 150 he had offended the gods. In mythology, seals were under the protection of Poseidon and Apollo because they symbolized the love of sea and sun. The monk seal is up to three metres long and weighs anything up to 340 kg. (260 kg. in the case of females). It lives about thirty or forty years and feeds on fish and octopus. An adult female usually gives birth to a single calf at the end of the summer, but not every year. The calf is weaned after about two months. Seals go ashore, in caves with a sand or shingle beach, to sleep and to give birth. The seal population in Greek waters has dwindled dramatically in recent years and the species is threatened with extinction in Europe as a result of over-fishing, contamination of the food chain and the development of tourism. It is now a protected species and international agreements are in place to try to ensure its preservation. There is a team of scientists based at Fiskárdo to observe and protect the seals.

151

Émblisi beach.

Walks: • **Ayía Efimía - Makriótika - Themáton Monastery - Ayia Efimía.** Uphill to the monastery. Follow the signposts. Time: 3 hrs.

• **Ayía Efimía - Neohóri - Ayia Efimía.** Uphill to Neohóri. Time: 4 hrs.

• **Fiskárdo - Tselendáta - Mánganos - Fiskárdo.** Start from the small jetty where boats are available for hire. The first part of the walk takes you past little coves ideal for swimming. Time: 4 hrs.

• **Fiskárdo - Émblisi beach - Fiskárdo.** A pleasant short walk for an afternoon bathe at Émblisi. Half-way along there is a taverna, but no refreshments are available at Émblisi beach. Time: 1 hr.

• **Fourniá peninsula - Émblisi beach.** A footpath signposted by the Fiskárdo Nautical and Environmental Club. Follow the signs, which start just after the harbour. Take water with you. Time: 1 hr.

• **Vassilikádes - Mesovoúnia - Playiá - Varí - Paliohérsou Monastery - Kothréas - Vassilikádes.** After Varí there is a signpost to the Paliohérsou Monastery. Time: 3 hrs.

152

Fiskárdo by night.

Useful phone numbers

Ayía Efimía
- Ayía Efimía Police Station: 2674 061 204
- Fire Brigade: 199
- Port Police: 2674 061 000
- Makriótika Doctor's Surgery: 2674 061 229
- Town Hall: 2674 061 207
- Taxis: 2674 061 114

For tourist information
- G.N.T.O.: 2671 022 248
- Ayía Efimía Police Station: 2674 061 204

Fiskárdo
- Fiskárdo Police Station: 2674 041 460
- Fire Brigade: 199
- Port Police: 2674 041 400
- Fiskárdo Doctor's Surgery: 2674 051 203
- Town Hall (at Vassilikades): 2674 051 181
- Taxis: 697 7713100 / 693 2637072

For tourist information
- G.N.T.O.: 2671 022 248
- Town Hall (Vassilikádes): 2674 051 181
- Fiskárdo Police Station: 2674 041 460

15

A taverna at Fiskárdo.

Argostóli - Thiniá district - Lixoúri

To get to Lixoúri from Argostóli you can either take one of the small ferries (frequent service, crossing time 25 mins.) or go by road, starting across the Drápanos bridge and then turning left and driving all round the Gulf of Argostóli.

From the villages of **Fársa** and **Kouroukláta** you get panoramic views over the Gulf of Argostóli: in fact Kouroukláta, which stands high up on a hill, is known locally as 'the balcony of Kefaloniá'. From there the road goes through the rocky farming district of Thiniá. The hill villages of **Kondogouráta**, **Kardakáta**, **Petrikáta**, **Nífi** and **Angónas**, on the foothills of Mt. Merovígli (988 m.), look west towards the Palikí peninsula. **Thiniá** produces a lot of olive oil, and another product for which it is well known is the local wine (*Thiniátiko krasí*), a red wine with a distinctive bouquet made from three varieties of grape, mainly Mavrodáfni. Ask in the villages where it can be bought. Two small beaches on the Thiniá coast are **Sotíra**, below Kondogouráta, and **Koumariá**, below Kardakáta. The road to Palikí turns left just after Kardakáta (straight on takes you to northern Kefaloniá).

The **Palikí** district covers the whole of the western peninsula of Kefaloniá: in antiquity this was the territory of the city-state of Pale. The Municipality of Palikí now has a population of 7,600 and Lixoúri, its main town, is the island's second biggest town. The Palikí peninsula, which is much lower and flatter than the rest of the island, consists of gentle hills whose clayey soil is excellent for agriculture, and the area produces large quantities of grain, olive oil, wine, vegetables and currants. Whichever way you turn, the landscape is rich with vineyards, cultivated fields, gardens and fruit trees. In the past Palikí was the granary of Kefaloniá and its inhabitants

Panoramic view of Lixoúri.

grew rich on the lucrative trade in grain and currants. It also grew a lot of flax and had a huge cottage industry of textile weaving. Nowadays the main local occupations, besides agriculture and tourism, are commerce, shipping and fishing. There is a large fish farm on the coast at Livádi.

Detail of a fresco at Angónas by the 'naive' painter Yerásimos Livadás.

Panoramic view of Livádi Bay.

Driving around Palikí, you will go through picturesque villages with large old houses and churches, all set in an endlessly green landscape. There are good tourist facilities in the area and several long sandy beaches.

Two kilometres after Kardakáta on the road to Lixoúri you come to a turning to the right which leads to **Zóla** and the long beach in **Ayía Kiriakí** Bay. Here it is worth trying some freshly-caught fish in one of the attractive seaside fish tavernas, enjoying the view along the coast of northern Kefaloniá while you eat.

After the Zóla turning, the main road descends into the **Livádi plain**. The coastal marshes here are ecologically important as a habitat of numerous species of wetland birds and plants. In spring and autumn these wetlands are visited by huge flocks of migrants that stop off in the Ionian Islands on their long aerial journeys, while graceful herons fish in the shallow waters of the Gulf of Argostóli. Eucalyptus trees have been planted round the edge of the marsh to keep mosquitoes away with the pungent smell of their leaves. A few kilometres beyond the ruins of the long-defunct agricultural prison, a turning to the right leads to the north coast of the Palikí peninsula at the picturesque Gulf of **Athéras**.

Continuing southwards along the main road, soon after **Kouvaláta** and **Áyios Dimítrios** you pass the locality known as Ritsáta. Near there on the left is 'Laskarátos's Hill', so called because the local satirical poet Andréas Laskarátos had a house there where he spent his summers. The house was rebuilt after the 1953 earthquakes by friends of the family. A minor road turning off to the left by a wayside shrine leads to the vineyards of the

156

Sklávos winery, where the grapes are grown organically. It produces Robóla and wines made from other varieties of grapes that are local to Palikí. The winery is open to visitors every evening (19:00-21:00).

Go back to the main road and turn towards Lixoúri, and after only twenty metres you come to a little old bridge – not visible from the car, as the modern road passes above it – connected with a local legend. In 1694 three Kefalonians were carried off by pirates and taken to the Barbary coast of North Africa. Shortly before 23rd August (the Apódosis or 'octave' of the feast of the Dormition of the Blessed Virgin) the three men thought nostalgically of the *paniyíri* held on that day at the Kechriónos Convent. The next day they were found alive and well, but still wearing their chains, under the little bridge not far from the convent. The chains are to be seen hanging from the throne of the Panayía Kechrionótissa in the conventual church.

Doúri Hill, a short distance before Lixoúri, was the acropolis of ancient Pale. Only scant remains of the Classical acropolis are now to be seen: ancient blocks of building stone were used in the construction of new buildings in Lixoúri in the seventeenth century, when the town was growing, because good quarry stone is in short supply in the relatively flat country round about.

Lixoúri stands on the east coast of the Palikí peninsula. The earliest written reference to the town occurs in a Venetian document of 1534, where it is called Lazuri. The town centre was (as it still is) on the waterfront, where the agricultural produce of Palikí was sold and shipped to Argostóli. The biggest factor in the development of Lixoúri was the currant trade, thanks to

157

The remote Glári beach in Ayía Kiriakí Bay, accessible only by boat.

which the town grew rapidly until the late eighteenth century. The most important building in the town was the Markátos Building, erected in 1824 by the British Resident Charles Napier to a design by the engineer J.P. Kennedy: it had shops on the ground floor and administrative offices and law courts above. Until 1844 Lixoúri was the biggest town on Kefaloniá, with 7,000 inhabitants, but in 1845 it was overtaken by Argostóli.

Lixoúri is now a small modern town that nevertheless still has something of the elegance and style characteristic of all towns in the Ionian Islands before the 1953 earthquakes. A seasonal torrent runs right through the middle of it and there are small bridges linking the northern and southern sections of the town. The people of Lixoúri are very proud of their town, which they like to call 'Little Paris', and they even refer to the river as 'the Seine'. In the old days the narrow streets would echo to the sound of the famous *kantadóri* (singers of *kantádes*). The *kantáda*, imported from Venice in the nineteenth century, is the type of popular song typical of Kefaloniá and the other Ionian Islands. Unlike the demotic songs of mainland Greece, which are monophonic, *kantádes* are sung in three-part harmony, to the accompaniment of a guitar or mandolin. It used to be common for men's voices to be heard singing in the streets in the evening or late at night, often outside a girl's window. They sang – often their own compositions – with spontaneous emotion, frequently improvising as they went along, and waited for the girl's reaction. *Kantadóri* were two a penny and their renderings were often superb. The older residents of the Ionian Islands still enjoy singing *kantádes*.

If you arrive at Lixoúri by ferry you will find yourself disembarking right in the middle of the waterfront. Nearby is the harbour for fishing boats and yachts. The long promenade with its flowerbeds and benches is a very pleasant place for an evening stroll. Alternatively you can sit over a coffee or an ice cream in the main square of Lixoúri, facing the harbour, which is surrounded on three sides by shops, tavernas and offices.

158

The primarólia (currants being loaded on to ships), 1920.

The cultivation of **currant vines** was introduced to the Ionian Islands from the Peloponnese. (The word 'currant' is derived from *Corinth*, from where currants were first exported to Western Europe.) Currant-growing in Kefaloniá expanded rapidly in the Venetian period, because it was a highly profitable business. Palikí, in particular, produced large quantities of high-grade currants. Grain farming declined dramatically all over the island, so much so that the Venetian Senate prohibited the planting of new currant vines, but the ban was ignored. The currants were transported in barrels from the quayside at Lixoúri to foreign ships anchored in the roads or in Argostóli harbour. The process of loading the currants on to ships is known locally as ***primarólia***. They were paid for partly in cash, partly in manufactured goods from northern Europe (e.g. textiles from England). The Venetians levied a tax on currant exports, which greatly increased their revenue, but the Kefalonians did not take this lying down and there was a flourishing contraband trade in currants smuggled out from the island's many small, remote bays. Since the beginning of the twentieth century there has been a steady decline in currant-growing.

As you walk round the town you will see statues of distinguished sons of Lixoúri, including Ilías Miniátis, Bishop of Kerkíni and Kalávrita; Stámos Petrítsis, a doctor and local benefactor; Yeóryios Typáldos-Iakovátos, a Radical member of the Ionian parliament; and the satirical poet Andréas Laskarátos. The statue of Laskarátos stands on the sea front, with his back to Argostóli. Some see this as a token of the rivalry, not to say enmity, that has bedevilled relations between Kefaloniá's two main towns for centuries. It dates back to 1757, when the Venetians moved the capital of the island from St. George's Castle to the then insignificant little port of Argostóli. The people of Lixoúri took this as a great insult, as their

159

Statue of Dr. Stámos Petrítsis.

160

Ioánnis Kapodístrias on a 500-drachma note.

town was developing strongly at that time. In 1797 matters came to a head and shots were fired in anger. In an attempt to restore peace, the Great Powers that controlled the island's destiny sent the young Ioánnis Kapodístrias, a native of Corfu who was then a diplomat in the Russian foreign service and was to become the first 'Governor' (President) of Greece in 1828, to mediate between the two factions and bring hostilities to an end. Kapodístrias spent some months in Kefaloniá, but his mission was a failure. The two towns now coexist in peace and harmony, and all that remains of the ancient rivalry is a constant interchange of jokes and good-natured banter. Until recently a cannon, nicknamed Carlos, was positioned in the main square of Lixoúri, pointing at Argostóli, but it has now been moved to the Platía Pessóndon, a nearby square whose name commemorates those killed in combat. The Kefalonian satirical poet Yeóryios Molféttas wrote an ode on the subject of the spectacular Easter celebrations at Lixoúri in 1900:

> *With such cannonades and fusillades,*
> *Such volleys fired in the air*
> *That you would have thought*
> *The fleet of Cervera was on fire....*

Finally Carlos thundered from the harbour entrance:

> *... And then a voice reverberated throughout Colombia*:*
> *'Boom out, Carlos, boom out, and let Argostóli be smashed!'*

One of the things worth seeing in the town is the carefully restored nineteenth-century house of the Typáldos-Iakovátos family, with beautifully decorated ceilings, that is now a public library (known as the Iakovátios Library) and museum. The library, on the ground floor, has a valuable collection of books that belonged to the Typáldos-Iakovátos family and the Alivizátos, Lambíris and Lovérdos families, all from Lixoúri. The Typáldos-Iakovátos collection comprises 6,500 volumes published between 1516 and 1890. Altogether the library contains 17,500 books, includ-

161

St. Mark and the beginning of his Gospel (3rd quarter of the 16th cent.). Iakovátios Library, Lixoúri.

*Colombia= Lixoúri

162

Detail of a ceiling in the Iakovátios Library.

ing a lending library of 9,000 newer books which are kept in the reading room. The first floor houses the museum and the manuscript collection, which includes parchment manuscripts of the Gospels from the thirteenth, fourteenth and fifteenth centuries, an early edition of Plato's complete works (Venice, 1556), paintings, antique furniture and icons of great value. The garden is used in summer for cultural events.

Opening hours: Tuesday-Friday 09:00-13:00, Saturday 09:30-12:00. Closed on Sundays and public holidays.

Lixoúri also has another library, the 'Damodós' Petrítsios Public Library endowed by Stámos Petrítsis, a local doctor. This has about 14,000 old books of all kinds, including some early editions printed in Venice and Leipzig.

What used to be the Valliánios Vocational Training School at Lixoúri, endowed by the Kefalonian benefactor Panayís Valliános, has recently been restored. Until the 1970s the school was renowned throughout Greece for its consistently high standards in various fields of vocational training. The buildings are now used as a state-run Technical College. Next to it is the recently-built town gymnasium.

Andréas Laskarátos (1811-1901) was born at Lixoúri. He read law at the Ionian Academy in Corfu and then went to Paris for further studies. On his return to Kefaloniá, at a time when the Ionian Islands were in a state of political and social upheaval, he settled down to write. A man of high moral principle, he believed it was his duty to inveigh against wrongdoing wherever he saw it. When his Mysteries of Kefaloniá was published in 1855, he was vilified as an atheist and excommunicated. The excommunication was not lifted until just before his death, when he was ninety years old and recognized as a great writer. Laskarátos is considered the greatest modern Greek satirical poet. A typical poem from his collection *Stichourgemata* (*Verses*) is the one entitled 'Why thalers are called thalers', in which he pokes gentle fun at the people of Lixoúri for their excessive pride in their town:

163

> *When God had created the world,*
> *Lixoúri and all those other places,*
> *He said to himself, 'So! All I need to do now,*
> *My son, is to create the people!'*

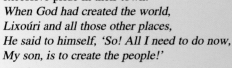

Some of the churches in Lixoúri contain magnificent carved wooden iconostases and icons. The town's patron saint is St. Harálambos, who is said to have saved the inhabitants from an outbreak of the plague. His feast-day on 10th February is celebrated with great pomp and ceremony, and his head is carried in precession through the streets.

The people of Lixoúri have the reputation of being clever, kind-hearted and sensitive. They enjoy jokes, dancing and singing, and all these characteristics are very much in evidence at the famed Lixoúri carnival before Lent, when crowds gather to be entertained by the procession of floats, the antics of the people in them, the dancing, music and satirical poems.

On big holidays and at other festivities the band of the Lixoúri Philharmonic School is always present. It also gives regular concerts all over Kefaloniá and in Athens as well. On 15th August the band plays in the Church of the Panayía tis Perlingoú in the town centre. Every evening from 1st to 15th August, before vespers, three flares are fired into the sky, and on the evening of the 15th, when the *paniyíri* is in full swing, the heavens are illuminated by a firework display.

For bathing from Lixoúri, the nearest place is the popular sandy beach of **Lépeda**, with crystal-clear water, where boats and canoes are available for hire.

The area south of Lixoúri is called Katoyí (Lowland) in contrast to the northern part of Palikí, which is called Anoyí (Upland). The road to **Manzavináta** and the **Katoyí** district passes through **Soullári** with its fine eighteenth-century Church of Ayía Marína, a scheduled historic monument. This and the Church of the Kímisis tis Theotókou at Rónghi (see below) are

The Philharmonic School, originally called the 'Music Company', was founded in 1836 by Pétros Skarlátos, who was its first principal. Skarlátos had studied under Livieri and Crica, both famous musicians in their day. The British authorities did not look kindly on the School, which rapidly developed into a 'hotbed of Radicalism'. In 1839 Skarlátos refused to play the British national anthem and the School was closed down. It reopened in 1855. Its achievements were officially recognized in 1864, when, at the ceremony to celebrate the union of the Ionian Islands with the rest of Greece, it became the first institution in the islands to be awarded a Greek flag woven with gold thread. The School maintains a band of over fifty musicians.

164

The band of the Lixoúri Philharmonic School.

165

Neoclassical Ionic pilaster in the Church of Ayía Marína, Soullári.

two of the four most important ecclesiastical buildings of recent times in Kefaloniá. An unusual feature of the Soullári church is the discrepancy between the two entrance doors: the one on the north side, which is older, is in Heptanesian Baroque style, while the one on the south is Neoclassical, with a triangular pediment and Ionic pilasters.

On the coast south of Soullári is the beautiful golden beach of **Mégas Lákkos**, where the bathing is excellent. The area round about is vine-growing country, where several well-known varieties of grape are grown (Mavrodáfni, Moscháto, Moschatélla, Vostilídi). You may like to try the local wines at the wine festival held every August at Manzavináta, where there is always a lively atmosphere and spontaneous dancing. Manzavináta is the home of the Vitorátos winery, one of six that have started up on the island in the last twenty years, producing Robóla and other wines (open daily to visitors, 10:00-14:00 and 18:00-20:00). From Manzavináta a road runs south to the lovely **Xi beach**, where the sand is reddish. Here watersports facilities are available and it is possible to hire a boat and cross over to the nearby islet of **Vardiáni**. For a long time there was a lighthouse on Vardiáni, 34 m. high(!), built by the British Resident Charles Napier to mark the west side of the four-kilometre-wide entrance to the Gulf of Argostóli. At **Akrotíri**, the southernmost point of Palikí, which was a port of call for mariners sailing to and from Italy and Sicily in antiquity, you can see the ***Kounópetra***, a logan-stone or rocking-stone, which attracts a great deal of interest: it is a large rock sticking up out of the sea, so delicately poised that it rocks to and fro. The movement is no longer as noticeable as it used to be. At **Vátsa** on the Akrotíri

166

Xi beach.

headland there was a sixth-century B.C. temple of Poseidon, the god of the sea. Today the site is occupied by the small Church of St. Nicholas, the patron saint of sailors, orphans and the poor. Part of the mosaic floor of the ancient temple, dating from the second century A.D., is to be seen in Argostóli Museum. Looking east along the coast from Akrotíri, you can see the distinctive white rocks overlooking Xi beach.

The village of **Vouní** was the birthplace of Yeóryios Bonános (1863-

1940), a sculptor with an international reputation. Bonános was a prolific sculptor in a Neoclassical style, producing work full of grace and harmony such as the Iakovátos monument and the statue of Stámos Petrítsis at Lixoúri, the statue of 'Soul' in the Drápanos cemetery and the marble fountain (not in use) in

167

Mosaic floor from the Temple of Poseidon at Vátsa.

168

The magnificent iconostasis of the Church of the Áyii Apóstoli at Havdáta.

169

Kipouréon Monastery (Monastery of the Annunciation at Kipoúria).

front of the Agricultural Bank of Greece in Platía Románou, Argostóli.

Beyond Vouní the road continues to **Havriáta**, a village surrounded by flat farmland and vineyards with a splendid view over the Ionian Sea. This was the home village of the philosopher Vikéntios Damodós (1679-1752), who studied in Italy. Damodós opened a school at Havriáta and taught there himself. He was one of the first scholars to use demotic Greek in philosophical writings, for he firmly believed that that was the only way for philosophy, scholarship and science to be made accessible to the general public. Near Havriáta is the house where the historian, folklorist and writer Ilías Tsitsélis spent his summers. Tsitsélis devoted his life to historical research and his monumental work *Kephallenian Miscellany* was published in 1904.

A turning to the left soon after Havriáta leads to the tall **Yero-gómbos** lighthouse and the pleasant beach of **Langadákia**, the nearest bathing-place to Havriáta.

The next village after Havriáta is **Havdáta**, the biggest village in the Palikí peninsula. The Church of the Áyii Apóstoli there has a superb eighteenth-century carved wooden iconostasis and some old icons. Unfortunately, most of the churches on Kefaloniá are closed on weekdays because of the risk of burglary. East of Havdáta the road passes by the small Convent of the Kímisis tis Theotókou Koronáton, set amid fields of vegetable and flower gardens.

After **Favatáta** and **Mandoukáta** a road off to the left climbs up to **Kaminaráta**, the highest village in Palikí, from where there are fantastic views to be had. Kaminaráta has a small museum of traditional arts and crafts, where it is worth looking at the old olive press. The road leading to the upper part of the village passes through farmland full of aromatic herbs, vineyards and olive-groves before arriving at the historic eighteenth-century Monastery of the Annunciation (Evangelismós tis Theotókou) at

170

The gate of the old Monastery of Ayía Paraskeví Taffon.

171

The eighteenth-century Church of the Kímisis tis Theotókou at Rónghi, near Monopoláta, a typical example of the Heptanesian style.

Kipoúria, generally known as the Kipouréon Monastery, which stands directly above the sea at the top of a ninety-metre cliff. In the monastery church there is an icon of the three most important saints of the Ionian Islands: St. Spyridon (the patron saint of Corfu), St. Gerásimos (Kefaloniá) and St. Dionysios (Zákinthos). The view from the monastery is magnificent, especially at sunset: the Ionian Sea appears to stretch away for ever, as there are no other islands to the west. Very near the monastery, on a hill 210 m. above sea level, are the ruins of the old Monastery of Ayía Paraskeví Tafíon, once a wealthy house with dozens of hectares of farmland. Its name alludes to the first known inhabitants of Kefaloniá and the neighbouring islands, the Taphioi. The water from the monastery spring is known for its medicinal properties against stomach complaints. Ancient coins and grave goods have been found in the vicinity. The road back to Lixoúri from here goes through Havriáta and Soullári.

Two kilometres before the Kipouréon Monastery there is a turning to the right leading to a viewpoint from which you can look down at the superb, long beach of **Platiá Ámmos**. At present the beach is only accessible by boat.

There are some lovely walks to be had around the hill villages of the **Anoyí** district, past picturesque old houses and historic churches and with an ever-changing panoramic view. At **Rónghi** on the road to **Monopoláta** it is worth stopping to look at an old privately-owned Baroque church (Church of the Kímisis tis Theotókou), which is one of the historic monuments of Kefaloniá. Next to it is a ruined mansion. To get to the church, park your car at the Mandoukáta-Monopoláta intersection and walk up the dirt road to the right.

The picturesque little villages of **Rífi** and **Damoulianáta** stand at an altitude of about 350 m. In the Anoyí district, which was once the biggest cereal-growing area on the island, you will see a lot of abandoned farmland. Windmills once used to grind the rich harvest of grain now stand in ruins around the countryside, defying the ravages of time, and an old millstone is now a feature of the village square at Damoulianáta. From there a minor road runs down through fields and olive-groves to the stunningly beautiful little beach of **Ayía Eléni**. From the square at Damoulianáta there is a spectacular view over the Ionian Sea at sunset.

The Byzantine Castle of St. George stood on the hill called Áyios Yeóryios, east of Rífi and Damoulianáta. The castle, surrounded by the rich farmland of the Palikí peninsula, was the administrative and ecclesiastical

172

The hamlet of Grekoussáta near Monopoláta.

capital of Kefaloniá until the end of the thirteenth century. Then, when the island's 'Frankish' rulers had interests in the Peloponnese, the castle near Argostóli took over from the one in Palikí, and later it took its name as well.

Between **Kaláta** and **Ayía Thékli** you will see the Keriá spring by the side of the road, where you can stop and quench your thirst. After Ayía Thékli and **Vilatória** there is a road off to the left to the long sandy beach of **Petaní**, one of the best in Kefaloniá, encompassed by cliffs at either end. Here you can hire a boat to go fishing, or simply to potter about in the waters of this exceptionally beautiful beach. Meals can be had at the seaside taverna.

In the charming village of **Kondoyenáda** stands the humble little Church of Áyios Yeóryios (12th-13th cent.), which is the oldest Christian monument on the island after the Early Christian basilica at Fiskárdo (see p. 119). Its priceless frescoes have been carefully removed and are kept elsewhere. Kondoyenáda was the birthplace of the internationally famous archaeologist Spyros Marinátos (1901-1974), who excavated a number of sites on Kefaloniá: in Palikí, at Mavráta in the Eliós district, at Lakíthra and at Mazarakáta in Livathó, among other places. His informative introduction to the history of Kefaloniá entitled *A Short Historical and Archaeological Sketch* is on sale in the Corgialenios Historical and Cultural Museum at Argostóli in a trilingual edition. Mycenaean tombs have been found near Kondoyenáda containing grave goods of considerable interest, including numerous vases, a stone larnax and small artefacts made of gold, bronze, stone, glass paste and clay. Some of them are on display in the Argostóli Archaeological Museum.

The road back to Lixoúri passes through the **Skiniá** area, where a yellowish limestone suitable for floors and ornamental work is quarried and processed. To return to Lixoúri, turn right at the Kechriónos Convent.

Walks: • **The hill villages of the Thiniá district**, starting from Kardakáta, then on down to the sea for a bathe at Sotíra or Koumariá beach. The long beach of Ayía Kiriakí, below Zóla, is also not far away.

• **Around the town of Lixoúri** - Typáldos-Iakovátos Library and Museum - Main Square.

• **Rífi - Damoulianáta - Ayía Eléni beach.** To walk round Rífi and Damoulianáta: 1 hr. The road down to Ayía Eléni starts from the square in Damoulianáta and takes you through olive-groves and vineyards, with fantastic views over the Ionian Sea. The last stretch down to the beach is very steep. No refreshments are available on the beach. Time from Damoulianáta to Ayía Eléni beach and back: about 3 hrs.

• The southern part of Palikí is good cycling country.

17

The sandy beach of Petaní.

Useful phone numbers

Lixoúri
- Lixoúri Police Station: 2671 091 207
- Fire Brigade: 199, Port Police: 2671 094 100
- Hospital: 2671 094 245
- Ayía Thékli Doctor's Surgery: 2671 097 208
- Post Office: 2671 091 206
- Town Hall: 2671 091 326
- Taxis: 2671 091524 / 2671 092 734
- Bus Station: 2671 093 200

For tourist information

- G.N.T.O.: 2671 022 248
- Tourist Police: 2671 022 815

Omalá valley - Convent of Áyios Yerásimos

The Omalá valley, roughly 10 km. from Argostóli, boasts the biggest and most prestigious monastic community on the island, the **Convent of Áyios Yerásimos**, which is the religious centre of Kefaloniá. The lovely Omalá valley, lying about 400 m. above sea level in the western foothills of Mt. Énos, is well watered by ground water from the mountain. There are also numerous wells, many of them said to have been dug by the convent's founder, Yerásimos Notarás, who was subsequently canonized and is now the island's miracle-working patron saint.

To reach Omalá, start out from Argostóli along the main Sámi road. After **Valsamáta** a straight stretch of road lined with poplars and cypresses leads to the imposing new church and the Convent of Áyios Yerásimos. By the gateway into the precinct there is a free-standing campanile in the Heptanesian style, as found next to many churches in Kefaloniá. The open spaces in the precinct are full of ornamental shrubs and flowers, tended by the nuns. In the conventual Church of the Panayía is a silver casket containing the body of St. Gerásimos. A staircase inside the church leads down to a small crypt which was his cell.

Icon of St. Gerásimos (19th cent.) in the ecclesiastical museum of Áyios Andréas Milapidiás.

174

The imposing new Church of Áyios Yerásimos on the Omalá plateau.

176

The wells dug by St. Gerásimos in the Omalá valley.

Yerásimos Notarás (1509-1579) came from an aristocratic family living at Tríkala, Korinthía. He became a monk at an early age and went to many parts of Greece before spending some time at Jerusalem, where he was ordained priest. On Kefaloniá he started living as a hermit in a cave in the Lássi district, at the place called Spília ('Caves'). Next he went to the Omalá valley, where he organized the Convent of Néa Ierousalím with thirty-two nuns. The new convent, built on the site of the old Convent of Ayía

177

The seventeenth-century iconostasis of the Church of the Panayía, by the Cretan wood-carver Moskétis. On the right is the silver casket containing the body of St. Gerásimos.

Ierousalím, was not only a religious centre but also a centre for cultural, educational and scholarly activities. One of the objectives St. Gerásimos set himself was to improve the educational standards of the nuns, and indeed of the islanders in general, and with that in mind he founded the nunnery's great library. It is interesting to note that the Italian scholar Letterio Augliera has recently published the results of research proving that one of the first printing presses in Greece was in this convent. When Gerásimos's corpse was exhumed for the removal of his bones to the ossuary, his body was found to be uncorrupted. He

178

was canonized by the Holy Synod of Constantinople in 1622. A great many miracles are attributed to the intercession of St. Gerásimos, mostly concerned with the exorcism of demons. He has two feast-days when his memory is celebrated by the Kefalonians with great pomp and ceremony: 16th August, the anniversary of his death, and 20th October, the anniversary of the translation of his relics. On both days his body is carried in procession from the large church to the well reputedly dug by him under a huge plane tree: it is always followed by thousands of Kefalonians and foreign visitors.

Early editions of religious books and some historic papyri are kept in the Mother Superior's quarters, and there is a guesthouse with accommodation for groups of visitors.

The Omalá valley and the country round about are the centre of the Robóla wine-growing area. Robóla – the wine for which Kefaloniá is most renowned, and indeed its best-known export of any kind – is a cool white wine with a fruity taste. The Robóla variety of grape does best on the thin, stony soil of the local mountainsides and can be grown up to 800 m. above sea level. In this inhospitable terrain, cultivation is hard work for the Kefalonian vine-growers. Since the grapes grow in rocky country, the Venetians called Robóla *Vino di sasso* ('wine of the rock'). Nowadays Kefaloniá produces about 600 tons of Robóla wine a year and has export markets in Europe, America and Japan. The Agroindustrial Cooperative, of Robóla Producers next door to the Convent of Áyios Yerásimos, produces other kinds of wine as well, and the Robóla vine-growers also supply grapes to other wineries on the island. The cellars of the Co-operative are open to visitors for wine-tasting and purchases (visiting hours: 08:00-21:00). Every August a Robóla festival is held in the Omalá valley: the atmosphere there is always lively, with music and dancing – and, of course, wine flowing freely.

Beyond the convent a minor road continues westwards and then southwards through never-ending vineyards of Robóla grapes. It takes you to the villages of **Troianáta, Demoutsandáta** and **Mitakáta** and passes below the foot of St. George's Castle before joining the main Argostóli-Póros road.

The Énos (Aínos) National Park

Fir cones.

At the 15th kilometre of the main road from Argostóli to Sámi there is a turning to the right which goes to the top of **Megálos Sorós** (1,628 m.), the highest peak of Mt. Énos. The Kefalonians call Mt. Énos *Megálo Vounó* ('Great Mountain') or simply *Vounó* ('Mountain'). Megálos Sorós is the highest peak in the Ionian Islands. The Énos range is a life-giving asset: huge tracts of land are watered by its seemingly inexhaustible aquifers. The protection of its natural environment is of crucial importance in maintaining the equilibrium of the whole island's ecosystem.

Since 1962 the mountain has been a national park, and as such it is protected by law. The main object of creating the national park was to protect the unique Cephalonian fir (*Abies cephalonica*, more commonly known as the Greek fir) and the rich native flora comprising some 350 different species of plants, shrubs and trees. The Énos fir forest, which starts at an altitude of 800 m., can properly be described as unique because nowhere else is there so large a forest of Cephalonian firs with the same degree of homogeneity.

Because the fir forests of Mt. Énos are so dark green as to look almost black, the Venetians called the mountain *Monte Nero* ('Black Mountain'). Such was its fame that when a Kefalonian named

The rare Poa mascula-russi *on Roúdi.*

Marínos Metaxás had an audience with Napoleon, the Emperor asked him how the famous forests of the Black Mountain were faring.

A trip up Mt. Énos is a must, if only to enjoy the spectacular view over the Ionian Sea and the mainland. Visibility is best on days when there is a breeze blowing and the clouds are not too low. Standing on the summit, you will see a map of the whole region spread out at your feet, with the Ionian islands of Lefkáda, Itháki and Zákinthos, the smaller islets in between and the shores of the Peloponnese and Central Greece. It is extraordinary how close the sea seems to be, when you are so far above it.

Owing to its geographical position, Mt. Énos has always been an important landmark for ships plying to and from the West. It has also been a key factor in the history and destiny of Kefaloniá and its people because of its valuable timber. References to the mountain are to be found in ancient literature, confirming that the wood of its fir trees was used in shipbuilding, and Homer uses the word 'firs' to refer to the oars of the Kephallenian ships. Scientific research has shown that the columns in the Minoan palace of Knossos were also made of fir. The profitable timber trade was thoroughly exploited by the island's later foreign rulers, such as the Romans and the Venetians: the latter actually established a colony of two hundred loggers at Omalá to keep their fleet and their castles supplied with timber, and forest rangers were appointed to prevent the local people from felling trees for their own use. The coins of the ancient city-state of Pronnoi, on the south-east slopes of the mountain, bore an image of a fir-cone, not found on any other ancient Greek coins.

Mt. Énos is connected with mythology and history as well as many local legends and traditions. In antiquity there was an altar of Zeus Ainesios, the father of gods and men, on the summit: traces of it can still be seen today. Its situation reminds us that the gods had their home on the summit of the highest mountain in Greece, Mt. Olympos.

The popular imagination has woven many curious stories around the dense, often impenetrable forest of Mt. Énos. The Venetian administration's official records for 1509 have preserved for posterity the thrilling legend of the 'gigantic winged dragon' that lived on the mountain and was in the habit of devouring human beings in the area around Áyios Nikólaos. All the efforts of the local inhabitants to kill the monster ended in failure, until finally two brothers named Brescani succeeded in overpowering and slaying it. The dragon was burnt outside the church of Áyios Nikólaos and the Brescani brothers were given large estates as a reward for their heroism.

181

Orchis quadripunctata *(four-spotted orchid)*.

182

Anemone blanda *(mountain windflower).*

Eminent European scientists have visited Kefaloniá for the purposes of geological and biological research. In the late nineteenth century Joseph Partsch, a German literary scholar and geologist, spent some years on the island. His studies on Kefaloniá and Itháki and his report on the 'Great Mountain' remain benchmarks for every scientist and historian studying the subject.

The forest has shrunk very considerably in the last few centuries as a result of catastrophic fires, and seedlings never grow to maturity because the sheep and goats grazing on the hillsides in their thousands consume everything in their path. Since 1962 all felling, grazing and other exploitation of the natural resources have been strictly forbidden within the boundaries of the national park in an attempt to protect and preserve this incomparable landscape. Special measures are also needed to ensure the survival of the wild horses that live on the mountain and are in danger of extinction: in the snows of midwinter they have to put up with very harsh conditions.

Walks in the National Park: • To Roúdi. After turning off the main Argostóli-Sámi road towards the summit, take the first forest road on the left. After 3 km. you have a panoramic view of the whole Sámi district: the town, the plain, the surrounding villages and the Gulf of Sámi, with Itháki and Lefkáda in the distance. Time: 2 hrs.

• **Harákti - summit of Mt. Énos - Harákti.** To get to Harákti (in the Piryí district), turn left off the Póros-Sámi road. Follow the forest road up the eastern slopes of the mountain. Two hours' walk brings you to an intersection where the road to the left goes to the village of Xenópoulo: keep right for the summit. From the summit a forest road leads down to the valley separating Énos from Roúdi. The road leading eastwards out of the valley brings you back to Harákti. Time: about 5 hrs.

Some facts about the Énos National Park

Total area: 2,862 hectares.
- Énos: 2,316 hectares, highest peak Megálos Sorós (1,628 m.).
- Roúdi: 546 hectares, highest peak Yoúpari (1,125 m.).

Bedrock:
Limestones formed in the sea 65-100 million years ago.

183

Flora and fauna (a representative selection)
- Principal tree: the unique Cephalonian fir, *Abies cephalonica*.
- Other trees and shrubs, chiefly on Roúdi: kermes oak, hawthorn, wild pear, holm oak, strawberry-trees (*Arbutus* spp.), Judas tree, mock privet (*Phillyrea* spp.), Jerusalem sage, wild roses, vines.
- Endemic plants: *Viola cephalonica*, *Saponaria aenesia*, *Scutellaria rubicunda* ssp. *cephalonica*, *Poa cephalonica*.
- Aromatic and medicinal herbs.
- Birds: blackbird, greenfinch, goldfinch, owls, rock partridge, larks, buzzard, griffon vulture, short-toed eagle.
- Reptiles: lizards, tortoises, adders.
- Small mammals: hedgehog, mole, weasel, stone marten, hare, fox.
- Small herds of wild horses live on the SE slopes of Mt. Énos.

184

Homer and Homeric Ithaka

185

The oldest known coin with an effigy of Homer (Ios, 4th cent. B.C.).

Homer's *Iliad* and *Odyssey*, the earliest literary treasures of the Western world, are thought to have been written in the eighth century B.C. Homer, in his inimitable, vivid language, describes events that took place in the Mycenaean period and provides us with valuable information about the Mycenaean world. For the ancient Greeks, these epics constituted a rich oral tradition full of memories of past times and packed with stories about the Olympian gods and other figures in Greek mythology. Homer's heroes get involved in fantastic adventures in various places in the Mediterranean, some of them familiar and some unidentified. With the gods pulling the strings to which they dance, they endure terrible sufferings and bring off amazing feats. All these elements, interwoven with such timeless human values as bravery, love and loyalty, ensure that Homer's epics have remained relevant right down to our own time.

The Iliad describes the last forty days of the Trojan War, which lasted ten years. The war was sparked off by the abduction of Helen, the beautiful wife of Menelaos, the Mycenaean king of Sparta, by Paris, son of the king of Troy. The Greeks gathered a great fleet and a great army and set off for Troy under the command of Agamemnon, king of Mycenae, to take revenge.

One of the heroes of the Trojan War was Odysseus (Ulysses), king of

Detail of the frieze from the sanctuary of Trysa in Lycia, Asia Minor (early 4th cent. B.C.). It depicts Penelope's suitors scrambling to avoid being slain by the arrows of Odysseus and Telemachos.

Ithaka, who broke the deadlock and gave victory to the Greeks by the ploy of the 'Trojan horse'. Odysseus was the ruler of the 'proud-hearted Kephallenians', whose domains included the islands off the west of Greece (except Corfu) and some coastal areas of Akarnanía and the Peloponnese. Consequently the kingdom centred on Kephallenia and Ithaka played a major part in the Western world's best-known mythological adventure.

The *Odyssey* describes the vicissitudes that befell Odysseus after the énd of the Trojan War. The eventful homeward journey of Odysseus and his companions took ten years because Poseidon, the god of the sea, who was angry with Odysseus, did everything in his power to prevent them from returning safely to Ithaka. Fortunately Odysseus had an ally in the goddess Athena.

187

'Melian relief' depicting Odysseus's reunion with Penelope after an absence of twenty years (c. 460-450 B.C.).

Through her intervention he eventually managed to return safe and sound to his beloved Ithaka after twenty years away, although all his companions met their deaths in the course of his misfortunes at sea. His wife Penelope, his son Telemachos and his father Laertes had virtually given up hope of ever seeing him alive. Old Laertes, widowed and grieving, had retired to his farm outside the city. The faithful Penelope was at her wits' end to fend off the many suitors from all over Odysseus's kingdom who had taken up residence in the palace. The suitors had decided to kill young Telemachos when he went to

188

Attic red-figure skyphos (two-handled drinking-cup), c. 445 B.C., with a painting of Telemachos with Penelope in front of her loom.

Nestor's palace at Pylos in search of news of his father. With Athena's help, Telemachos escaped certain death and came back unharmed to the city of Ithaka, having avoided the ambush which the suitors had laid for him on the islet of Asteris on his return from Pylos. At this critical juncture, when hope had almost died and the suitors seemed to be closing the net round Penelope and Telemachos, Odysseus finally arrived back in Ithaka. With Telemachos, and with Athena's help once again, he managed to outwit and kill the suitors and restore order in his kingdom.

The events described in the *Iliad* and *Odyssey* are not mere figments of Homer's literary imagination: they are based on

18

'Ulysses and the Sirens' (Herbert Draper, 19th cent.). In Draper's free rendering of the scene, the Sirens are actually aboard Odysseus's ship. The oarsmen plugged their ears with wax to make themselves deaf to the seductive singing of the Sirens, while Odysseus had himself lashed to the mast.

historical reality. In the second half of the nineteenth century the German archaeologist Heinrich Schliemann, using Homer as his guide, set out to find Homeric Ithaka. He conducted the first excavations on Itháki in 1868 but failed to find Odysseus's palace. However, he did succeed in discovering the city of Troy and the royal tombs at Mycenae and Orchomenos.

The location of Odysseus's capital is still a matter of dispute among historians and archaeologists even today, and hundreds of different theories on the subject have been published in the last 150 years. The German archaeologist Wilhelm Dörpfeld caused a great stir early in the twentieth century when he advanced the theory that Homeric Ithaka was actually the island of Leukas (Lefkáda), and since then others have stirred up a hornets' nest by suggesting that the capital of Odysseus's kingdom was on Kefaloniá. The discovery and excavation of a Mycenaean tholos tomb at Tzannáta, near Póros in south-eastern Kefaloniá, near the end of the twentieth century, sparked off a new round of books and articles, debates and polemic on this controversial topic. When all is said and done, the quest for Homer's Ithaka and the resulting arguments have drawn attention to the common heritage shared by all the territories of Odysseus's ancient kingdom.

190

'The Apotheosis of Homer' (Ingres, 19th cent.).

As you set out for Ithaka,
hope the voyage is a long one,
full of adventure, full of discovery.
....
Keep Ithaka always in your mind.
Arriving there is what you are destined for.
But do not hurry the journey at all.
Better if it lasts for years,
so you are old by the time you reach the island,
wealthy with all you have gained on the way,
....

C.P. Cavafy (1863-1933,

19

ITHÁKI

FACTS ABOUT
ITHÁKI AND
THE ITHAKANS

Panoramic view of Vathí, with Lazarétto islet in the background. 192

Geographical position - Size - Population

Itháki, the fifth biggest of the Ionian Islands, has an area of 96 sq.km. It lies very close to the eastern and north-eastern shores of Kefaloniá. To the north lies Lefkáda, to the east the coast of Akarnanía and the small uninhabited islets called the Echinádes. Kefaloniá and Itháki are separated by a strait about 22 km. long. The Gulf of Mólos carves a deep indentation on the east side of Itháki, effectively dividing it into a northern and a southern part joined by the Aetós isthmus, which is a mere 620 m. wide.

Like Kefaloniá, Itháki is a mountainous island, rising to just over 800 m. above sea level at the summit of Mt. Nírito, and flat land is at a premium. There are very few natural springs, but the wet winters – a characteristic feature of the climate on the west coast of Greece – support lush vegetation.

Itháki is part of the Prefecture of Kefaloniá and Itháki. The whole island constitutes a single municipality with a population of about 3,000, of whom 1,800 live in the main town, Vathí.

Pretty orchards and olive-groves alternate with the beauty of untamed nature, making Itháki a place of amazing contrasts. Small though the island is, its jagged coastline is about 100 km. long, with beautiful beaches and delightful coves.

The flora and fauna are similar to those of Kefaloniá. Offshore, the loggerhead sea turtle (*Caretta caretta*) and the Mediterranean monk seal (*Monachus monachus*) are sometimes seen. Their populations are much smaller than in Kefalonian waters, but here too you may come across clutches of turtles' eggs buried in the sand.

The island's principal agricultural products are olive oil, wine and honey. Other economic activities are stockbreeding, commerce, fishing and, in the last few decades, tourism. Many of the young men join the merchant navy.

In the age-old tradition of the Ionian Islanders, the people of Itháki are very musical. They also love the theatre (there is a flourishing dramatic society in the town) and the arts generally. They are passionately devoted to their island, but fate has decreed that most of them spend their lives far from home, for emigration in the last two hundred years has scattered them to 'the round earth's imagined corners'. The Ithakans are known all over the world for their commercial acumen and their seamanship.

Tourism is increasing steadily and has become a major source of income for the local people. The hotels and other tourist facilities are very well positioned and their standards will not disappoint even the most demanding customer. Because the distances are so small it is easy to tour the whole island, no matter where you stay, and you will certainly fall in love with Itháki and the Ithakans at first sight.

The history of Itháki and its people

Various explanations have been given for the origin of the name 'Ithaka' or 'Itháki', one being that Ithakos and his brothers, the sons of Pterelaos, were the first settlers on the island. From the eleventh century it was known to Western Europeans as Cefalonia Piccola ('Little Cephalonia'), Anticefalonia (the island opposite Cephalonia) or Val di Compare (*compare* being a type of ship). All these names went out of use in the eighteenth century. Nowadays the local people use the name Thiáki for the island and Thiakós for an Ithakan.

The history of Itháki is closely bound up with that of Kefaloniá and the other Ionian Islands. The earliest archaeological finds attesting to human habitation come from the northern part of the island and have been dated to the third millennium B.C. It is not known when the first inhabitants settled there.

Interesting finds and evidence of organized life in the prehistoric era (3000-2000 B.C.), such as roads and walls, have been discovered on Pilikáta hill near Stavrós in the north of the island. Ancient artefacts of the Pre-Mycenaean period (2000-1500 B.C.) and later periods have been found in the Loízou Cave on Pólis Bay (Órmos Póleos), also near Stavrós. Objects of Mycenaean date have been found at Stavrós and Tris Langádes.

In the eighth century B.C. Ithaka, like Akrotíri in the Palikí district of Kefaloniá, was used by the Corinthians as a port of call for mariners sailing to and from Sicily and southern Italy, and trade stimulated the island's development. The hill above Aetós was probably the site of the city of Alalkomenai, the remains of which are still visible.

In 180 B.C. the Romans conquered the Ionian Islands, including Ithaka. In the Byzantine period, from the fifth century onwards, the Ionian Sea was infested with marauding Vandals from Africa, Goths from Europe and, later, Saracen (i.e. Arab) and Slav pirates. The islanders were at risk from pirate raids until the eighteenth century. Sarakíniko, the name of a cape and bay on the east coast of Itháki, preserves the memory of the Saracen corsairs who took over the area and had a hide-out there. Arab corsairs were the scourge of the Mediterranean, looting and pillaging on a large scale. It has to be said that the Ithakans, like the Kefalonians, were not always on the receiving end, for they, too, took to piracy in a big way. After 1450 the Spanish sent a combined naval and military force to blockade Itháki because the islanders were attacking and robbing all shipping in the channel

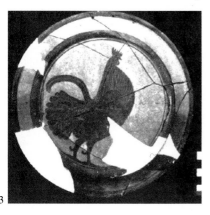

193

Corinthian plate of the 6th cent. B.C., found in the Loízou Cave in 1930.

between Kefaloniá and Itháki. Eventually they overcame the defenders' opposition and devastated the island in reprisal.

Until the Venetians took possession of Itháki in 1500, living conditions were extremely harsh. The first concern of the new Venetian administration was to increase the population, so in 1504 a decree providing for the resettlement of the island was issued. Settlers were brought in from mainland Greece and whole families were moved there from the other Ionian Islands, being rewarded with free grants of land and special tax exemptions. As a result of this policy, the population had risen to about 10,000 by the end of the Venetian period (1797). The development of trade and the growth of the Ithakan merchant fleet brought an improvement in living conditions. The Venetians encouraged olive-growing on a commercial scale, with the result that for many years olive oil and

194

The Cyclopean walls on the hill at Aetós. From William Gell, The Geography and Antiquities of Ithaca, *1806.*

19

View of Itháki harbour with British warships, by the English artist Joseph Cartwright (1789-1829). It shows an armed British soldier, Ithakans in baggy breeches and a boat arriving from Lazarétto. The passenger in the bows of the boat is giving something to a person behind bars, who takes it from him with a pair of tongs. Presumably it is a letter from someone in quarantine. Before being delivered to their addressees, letters were fumigated to kill any germs they might be carrying.

currants were the island's main exports. There was also a modest trade in oak wood.

The French occupation of Itháki lasted until 1799, when a Russo-Turkish fleet seized the island. Under the Treaty of Constantinople (1800) between Russia and Turkey, the Ionian Islands were recognized as an integrated state to be known as the Septinsular Republic, under the suzerainty of the Sultan of Turkey. The protection given by the Sultan to Heptanesian shipping, combined with the collapse of Venetian maritime supremacy, led to the development of trade and the growth of the Ithakan merchant fleet, for the Ithakans had always been a seafaring people. During this period one out of every three Ithakan men was a sailor in an Ithakan or foreign ship!

Col. William M. Leake, a British traveller who went to Itháki in 1806, tells us a lot about the Ithakan merchant fleet in his book *Travels in Northern Greece*. Out of 8,000 Ithakans, he says, about 1,200 lived outside the island, most of them in Constantinople. Some were merchants, importing grain and ore from the Black Sea; others were seamen working on Ithakan vessels owned by those same merchants; and most combined the two occupations. Ithakans owned about fifty sailing ships manned by local crews and the same number of caiques for trade with the neighbouring islands. The Romanian historian Nicolae Iorga, author of *The History of the Romanians*, writes: *Small-scale as well as large-scale commerce in our country began with the Greeks who came from the Ionian Islands: the Kefalonians and, more particularly, the Ithakans.*

Itháki was brought under British protection in 1815. British government policy at that time was pro-Turkish and the British administrators in the islands discouraged any kind of participation by the local people in the Greek rebellion against the Turks. The islanders refused to be intimidated, however, and they gave a great deal of support to the Greek side in the War of Independence, which broke out in 1821. The Ithakans used their ships to transport provisions and matériel and offered their island as a safe haven for revolutionaries wanted by the Turks. One of the great figures in the War of Independence, Odysséas Androútsos, was born on Itháki. The British protectorate came to an end in 1864, when the Ionian Islands were united with the rest of Greece. The most prominent Ithakan Radical was Tilémachos Paízis, a staunch advocate of union with Greece.

196

Coins of the British protectorate. Left: the winged lion of Venice holding a closed Gospel book with seven arrows between its pages. Right: Britannia with the trident symbolizing Britain's maritime supremacy.

When the British left Itháki the island had about 15,000 inhabitants, but the steady exodus of migrants in the nineteenth and twentieth centuries led to a dramatic decline in the population. The remittances sent home by seamen and emigrants helped their families to maintain a decent standard of living. Today, the biggest Ithakan community outside Greece is in Melbourne, Australia. Emigrants and their families often come back to their home island in the summer, combining a holiday with a return to their roots and the old traditions.

During this period of political and social change in the nineteenth and early twentieth centuries, Itháki found its way on to the itineraries of many travellers, mostly from northern Europe. At that time the influence of ancient Greek civilization was widely felt in Europe, in science, art and architecture. Homer was read at school and university, books about ancient Greece poured off the presses, great artists painted pictures of scenes from Greek mythology, Neoclassical public and private buildings sprang up everywhere. It has to be said, though, that not all travellers came to Greece with the purest of motives. Archaeology as a science was then in its infancy and there were no laws for the protection of the country's ancient heritage, with the result that thefts of antiquities were a commonplace occurrence. Ancient works of art of incalculable value are now to be found scattered all over the world, in private and public collections.

The name of Ithaka exerted a powerful attraction on foreign travellers. The Englishmen Leake and Gell, the Germans Schliemann and Dörpfeld, the Frenchman Victor Bérard and the Dutchman Adriaan Goekoop are just some of the eminent figures who visited Itháki. Most of them were determined to identify the island as the place described by Homer and to discover the palace of the mythical Odysseus. The first attempts to identify Itháki with Homer's Ithaka were made by the Englishmen William Gell and William Martin Leake in the early years of the nineteenth century. After studying the island's physical features, Gell came to the conclusion that the Mycenaean city was at Aetós (the probable site of ancient Alalkomenai). Leake maintained that it was in the north of the island, at Stavrós. Some years later, the Greek archaeologist Fílippos Ikonómou suggested a third possible site at

197

A traditional Ithakan costume.

Voúnos, south-east of the town of Vathí. Heinrich Schliemann visited Itháki twice and made some trial excavations on the hill at Aetós, but failed to find what he was hoping for. A hundred and fifty years later, excavations are still under way in various parts of the island under Ioánnis Papadópoulos and Sarándis Simeónoglou. Every two years the Centre for Odyssey Studies, based at Vathí, organizes an international conference on Homeric topics, and seminars on Homer's work and the relevant literature are held every year for teachers of Greek from all over the country. Ithaka, the homeland of Odysseus, is generally regarded as the universal symbol of the best kind of patriotism and love of one's home, a combination of sentiments that Homer expresses so brilliantly in the person of Odysseus.

198

Portrait of Heinrich Schliemann (Sidney Hodges, 1877).

A TOUR OF THE ISLAND

Panoramic view of Kióni.

Vathí

Vathí, the island's main town, is set amphitheatrically on the slopes surrounding a landlocked arm of the beautiful **Gulf of Mólos**. The name means 'Deep', and the town is so called because the bay makes such a deep indentation in the coastline. After the 1953 earthquakes the houses were rebuilt in the old traditional style of the Ionian Islands, and in 1982 the town was officially designated a 'traditional settlement', which means that any new buildings erected must conform to strict design specifications.

The port of Vathí has regular ferry connections with Kefaloniá and Pátra. In summer there are always dozens of yachts moored at the quayside or

anchored offshore. The tiny islet in the bay is called Lazarétto, because it was the quarantine station during the Venetian period: the fear of epidemics was ever-present, and the passengers and crews of foreign vessels were kept on the islet for 30-40 days before being allowed ashore. The word *lazaretto*, meaning a quarantine station, is derived from the Chapel of Santa Maria di Nazaret, a monastery chapel on the canal of the same name in Venice, where the first quarantine station was built in 1423. For centuries this was taken as the model for all quarantine stations in Europe. After the departure of the Venetians Lazarétto island was used as a prison until the end of the nineteenth century. The only building on the island now is the little Church

201

The Vathí agricultural show.

of the Sotíras. During the second French occupation (1807-1809) the French, expecting to be attacked by the British, built two small forts flanking the entrance to the harbour to protect the town: their ruins are still visible.

The hub of Vathí's social life is the main square, lined with cafés, tavernas and bars. Shops, the bank, the post office and the town hall are in the streets round about. The shops are well stocked with local produce such as olive oil, wine and fruit preserves, and you can also buy these and other local products, such as embroideries, at the annual agricultural show in August. In summer there are a number of theatrical performances, art exhibitions and other cultural events. The town band plays in the main square of Vathí and in the villages at local festivals. Accommodation is available in tourist hotels in and around the town.

The Itháki Cultural Centre has a room used for lectures, recitals and film shows. Its library contains a number of rare books, including old editions of the Odyssey and Iliad.

In the middle of the town there are two museums, the Archaeological Museum and the Maritime and Folk Art Museum. The **Archaeological Museum** has a collection of finds (pottery, bronzes and coins) from the excavations on the hill at Aetós, spanning the centuries from the Geometric to the Roman period (800 B.C. - A.D. 300). Do not miss the votive plaque with the names of Athena and Hera that was found in the Loízou Cave in the north of the island (c. 600 B.C.).

Opening hours: Tuesday-Sunday 08:00-15:00. Closed on Mondays and public holidays.

The **Maritime and Folk Art Museum** is in a restored building. It contains exhibits connected with the islanders' everyday life, such as furniture, portraits and old musical instruments, as well as nautical equipment used in the days of sail.

Opening hours: Monday - Saturday 9:30-15:30. Closed on Sundays, open on public holidays.

The Metropolis (Cathedral) of Itháki, dedicated to the Presentation of the Blessed Virgin, contains an exquisite old carved wooden iconostasis. In the Church of Áyios Nikólaos there is a superb icon of Christ, thought to be by El Greco.

One of the very fine old houses in the town, the Drakoúlis house, is an imposing Neoclassical building with Ionic columns and a small pond. In the 1930s the London-based shipping company Dracoulis Ltd., then under the

202

The Drakoúlis house.

management of Pericles Dracoulis, an Ithakan, signed an agreement with the rising young shipowner Aristotle Onassis, in whose ships hundreds of Ithakan seamen sailed during the next few decades.

In the Gulf of Mólos you can bathe at **Tsirimbí** and **Loútsa** beaches. Further away from Vathí are the sandy beaches of **Mnímata**, **Skíno**, **Filiatró** and **Sarakíniko**. If you have not brought a car, you can get around the island by bus or taxi; alternatively, boats can be hired in Vathí harbour.

203

Yidáki beach.

Southern Itháki

A few kilometres south of Vathí is the one and only village in southern Itháki, the picturesque **Perahóri**, set amid olive and oak trees on Petaléiko hill, on the slopes of **Mt. Merovígli** (671 m.), with a fantastic view over the sea. Perahóri is noted for its wine, and every year at the end of July there is a wine festival there with music and dancing. The tavernas serve meat baked in the traditional way in a clay pot called a *tserépa*, which is placed in glowing coals and left until the meat is cooked. In the Venetian period this was the most densely populated part of the island: the main village then was what is now called **Paleohóra** ('Old Village'), above Perahóri. Nothing is left from that period except some derelict churches with amazing frescoes and the ruins of some medieval houses. Little by little, the inhabitants moved to Vathí when it started growing in the sixteenth century, and those that did not go to Vathí moved to what is now Perahóri.

The seventeenth-century Taxiarchón Monastery (Monastery of the Taxiarchs, i.e. the Archangels Michael and Gabriel), no longer in use, lies south-west of Perahóri at an altitude of 500 m. The only oak woods still remaining on the island are at Afendikós Lóngos, to the west.

In the Marathiás area, on the east coast of southern Itháki, there is a beautiful little beach with the islet of **Péra Pigádi** just offshore. This part of the island has been identified by some scholars as the area where the swineherd Eumaios took Odysseus's pigs to graze, near the spring of Arethousa and the Raven's Crag.

The coastal road from Vathí to Píso Aetós and northern Itháki starts off along the shore of the Gulf of Mólos, with splendid views across the water. Before you get to Píso Aetós, you pass the popular beach of **Dexá**, where you can hire boats, canoes and pedalos. Shortly before Dexá a path goes up to the left to the **Marmarospiliá** or **Cave of the Nymphs**, which contains a fine display of stalactites and stalagmites in a variety of shapes and colours.

A wayside shrine at Paleohóra.

205

The islet of Péra Pigádi off southern Itháki.

According to local tradition this is the 'Cave of the Nymphs whom men call Naiads' near the harbour of Ithaka, mentioned by Homer. The cave has been developed for tourism and is open daily, 09:00-21:00.

Píso Aetós has a beach and a small harbour from which there are ferry services to Sámi, Fiskárdo and Lefkáda. The lovely beach of **Mbros Aetós** is popular with swimmers and fishermen. On the hill above Aetós are the ruins of an ancient city (8th cent. B.C.), where there was probably a temple of Apollo. The ruins are known locally as 'Odysseus's Palace'.

206

Aetós archaeological site.

Northern Itháki

The beach of Áspros Yalós at Ái-Yánnis.

At the end of the Aetós isthmus a turning to the right off the main road leads to the **Katharón Monastery**, situated on a shelf of level ground on the slopes of **Mt. Nírito**, 556 m. above sea level. The monastery is dedicated to the Panayía Kathariótissa, the patroness of the island. Founded in the seventeenth century and completely rebuilt after the 1953 earthquakes, it is the religious centre of Itháki. The monastery church contains some fine frescoes and an old wood-carved iconostasis. The panoramic view from the bell-tower is breathtaking: spread out before you are Kefaloniá, the Gulf of Mólos, the Echinádes islands, the Gulf of Pátra and the mountains of Lefkáda and Akarnanía. If you are on Itháki in September, do not miss the *paniyíri* at the Katharón Monastery on 8th September.

From the monastery the road continues to the highest village on Itháki, Anoyí (520 m.). **Anoyí** was once the island's main town, when the villages were built on hills well away from the sea as a precaution against pirate raids. The very old Church of the Panayía at Anoyí, with excellent Byzantine frescoes of the late seventeenth century and an iconostasis with paintings by G. Agrafiótis, is a listed building. The Venetian campanile stands some distance away from it, so that the church should not be damaged if the campanile were brought down by an earthquake. The key of the church can be obtained from the nearby café. Above modern Anoyí are the ruins of the old village, as at Perahóri. Just outside Anoyí there are two huge monoliths

208

The monolith called Arákli, near the school at Anoyí, is 8 metres high.

standing sentinel: one is called Kaval-láris ('The Horseman') and the other Arákli (a corruption of Herakles). To the east of the village the mountain plunges steeply down to the stretch of coast that includes Kióni Bay and Mavrónas Bay. To the north it is more of a plateau, sloping much more gently. For centuries the villagers of Anoyí scratched a hard living from the poor soil by terracing the mountainside with miles of stone retaining walls. The principal crops were cereals.

From Anoyí a road winds down to **Stavrós**, the biggest village in northern Itháki. Enjoy the view, but mind the bends! Stavrós can also be reached by the main road into northern Itháki, which runs parallel to the tree-clad west coast but fairly high above the sea, with good views across to northern Kefaloniá. Soon after leaving the Aetós isthmus by this western road you will get your first view of **Léfki**, a village clinging to the precipitous west slope of Mt. Nírito, where there is a limited amount of accommodation available in rented rooms. From there a road runs down to the delightful beach of **Áspros Yalós** and the hamlet of **Ái-Yánnis**. From Stavrós you can see down to both the west and the east coast of the island. In the middle of the village there are shops and tavernas, as well as the fine old Church of the Sotíras and a bust of Odysseus. A number of traditional-style old houses are still standing and in use.

20

Seventeenth-century frescoes in the Church of the Panayía at Anoyí.

Half an hour's walk from Stavrós brings you to peaceful **Pólis Bay** (Órmos Póleos), used as an anchorage by fishing boats and yachts. On the north shore of the bay is the Loízou Cave, named after the man who discovered it, which yielded major finds proving that it was used as a shrine

210

Pólis Bay (Órmos Póleos).

The area around Stavrós has been inhabited continuously since the end of the third millennium B.C. and is of considerable archaeological interest. The **Loízou Cave** on Pólis Bay, the village of **Stavrós**, **Pilikáta hill** and the 'School of Homer' at **Áyios Athanásios** are major archaeological sites. Excavations have brought to light ancient fortifications, settlements, tombs, tools, household utensils, cult idols, coins and jewellery. In the 1930s the British School at Athens excavated at all the sites mentioned above and at Píso Aetós, with funding from the English diplomat and amateur archaeologist Sir Rennell Rodd. The Ithakans themselves, too, have raised funds privately to finance excavations. Some of the finds are now in the British Museum. Many of the sites in this part of the island have been provisionally identified as places mentioned by Homer. The **Stavrós Archaeological Museum** contains many of the finds from the excavations in northern Itháki, including a fragment of a clay female mask of the second or first century B.C. with the inscription ΕΥΧΗΝ ΟΔΥΣΣΕΙ ('a votive offering to Odysseus') found in the Loízou Cave, attesting to the existence of a cult of Odysseus in late antiquity.

Opening hours: Tuesday-Sunday 08:30-15:00. Closed on Mondays and public holidays.

211

212

The village of Exoyí, clinging to the mountainside, commands a view over Afálon Bay.

in antiquity. On the beach you can relax in the shade of a big plane tree, enjoying the unspoilt surroundings.

From Stavrós there is a choice of roads: one goes to Exoyí, one to Platrithiás and one to Fríkes and Kióni. **Exoyí**, the most northerly village on the island, stands high on the mountainside with wide views over the sea. Its position makes it an excellent vantage point, and in the Middle Ages it was one of the biggest villages on Itháki. From **Pernarákia** you can survey the whole majestic expanse of the Ionian Sea. The deserted Monastery of the Panayía is at Pernarákia. Rooms are available to rent at Exoyí.

Platrithiás stands amid fertile green farmland, with its satellite hamlets of **Lahós**, **Kálamos**, **Mesovounó**, **Áyii Saránda** and **Kolierí**. Not much damage was done here by the 1953 earthquakes, so there are still a good many traditional-style old houses to be seen. Rooms are available to rent at Platrithiás, which is the headquarters of the Olive-Growers' Co-operative for the surrounding district. Near Platrithiás are Afálon Bay and Fríkes Bay. **Afálon Bay** is very beautiful and an ideal spot for swimming and fishing. At Kolierí, 1 km. north of Platrithiás, there is an open-air museum of traditional crafts with an old olive press. The largest natural spring on Itháki is at the now uninhabited hamlet of Kálamos: its waters are used to irrigate the whole plain down to Afálon Bay.

The village of **Fríkes**, on the east coast, lies in a narrow valley. It was founded in the seventeenth century by people who moved there from Exoyí and Stavrós, and its natural harbour provided shelter for boats trading with Lefkáda and the mainland. In summer the harbour is full of yachts, and it is a port of call on the one-day cruises

213

The Church of Áyios Nikólaos at Exoyí.

214

The open-air museum of traditional crafts in the little square at Kolierí. The old farm implements and millstones preserve the memory of generations of Ithakan farm workers.

from Kefaloniá to Itháki. In the village you can find rooms in the hotel or in guesthouses, and fish tavernas for your meals, Fríkes Bay being a well-known fishing-ground. There is a beach at Fríkes and others not far away at **Liménia** and **Kourvoúlia**. Ferries run from there to Lefkáda. Some scholars believe that Fríkes Bay was the harbour of Rheithron, mentioned by Homer as being near the city of Ithaka.

From Fríkes to Kióni is a scenic drive that takes you past numerous coves with sapphire-blue water and small beaches. In **Mavrónas Bay**, before you reach Kióni, is the chapel of Áyios Nikólaos, one of the oldest churches on the island; there was once a monastery on the site. The pretty village of **Kióni**, now officially classified as a 'traditional settlement', was founded by people from Anoyí, and the old mulepath between the two is still in existence. On the left side of the bay you can see some of the typical old houses. In the nineteenth century Kióni was a busy port with a population of about a thousand and the verdant countryside round about was full of olive trees – so much so that Kióni village alone had no less than ten olive presses. The first steamship to serve Itháki, the *Ithakos*, was owned by businessmen from Kióni and plied between Fríkes, Kióni and Vathí. Nowadays the picturesque village with its sheltered harbour and landlocked bay is popular with yachtsmen, and the tourist traffic gives the place an air of cheerful liveliness. Boats can be hired at the harbour to take you to the nearby beaches of **Katsikoúli**, **Sarakinári** and **Plakoútses**. Accommodation is available in rented rooms or holiday apartments. To get back to Vathí you have to retrace your steps via Stavrós.

For a pleasant walk with beautiful views of the countryside, set off along the path from **Filiatró beach** that leads to three typical old windmills and the east side of Argaliós hill. Beyond the windmills is the seaside chapel of Profítis Ilías: on 20th July, the feast-day of the Prophet Elias (Elijah), crowds of people go there from Kióni to attend the Divine Liturgy before returning to the village for a *paniyíri* in the evening.

215

The Mármaka area and the northernmost shores of Itháki.

216

The village of Kióni, officially classified as a 'traditional settlement'.

21

Fríkes.

218

The Mármaka area and the northernmost shores of Itháki.

Useful phone numbers

Vathí
- Police Station: 2674 032 205
- Fire Brigade: 2674 033 199
- Port Authority: 2674 032 909
- Health Centre: 2674 032 222
- Post Office: 2674 032 386
- Town Hall: 2674 032 795
- Taxis: 2674 033 030
- Bus Station: 2674 032 104

Stavrós
- Post Office: 2674 031 209
- Doctor's Surgery: 2674 031 207

For tourist information

- G.N.T.O.: 2671 022 248
- Vathí Town Hall: 2674 032 795
- Police Station: 2674 032 205

GENERAL BACKGROUND INFORMATION

Religion and the Church

The overwhelming majority of Greeks belong to the Eastern Orthodox Church. In Greek Orthodox churches you will see no statues but a lot of icons and wall-paintings of saints and Biblical scenes painted in Byzantine style, often with traces of Italian Renaissance influence.

Three major feast-days falling close together in winter are Christmas, New Year's Day (the feast of St. Basil the Great) and the Epiphany. Special kinds of confectionery and bread are made in the Christmas season. It is on New Year's Day that presents are given to the children and a special cake (the *vassilópita*) is baked with a lucky coin inside it. On Christmas Eve and New Year's Eve groups of children go from house to house singing the *kálanda* (traditional carols offering seasonal greetings to the household) to the accompaniment of a triangle. In the old days they would be given treats to eat, but now it is usually money. On the very last days of the year it is customary to play gambling games, especially card games such as poker. The feast of the Epiphany (6th January) commemorates Christ's baptism by John the Baptist in the River Jordan. This is the day when the waters are blessed: in harbours and other places on the coast the priest throws a cross into the sea and young men dive in to retrieve it.

The carnival season, called the *máskara* on Kefaloniá, lasts for four weeks before the beginning of Lent, and almost everybody joins in the festivities. The streets are full of people in fancy dress going to the celebrations held in village squares, with eating, drinking and merrymaking. In the Orthodox Church Lent begins on a Monday, known as Clean Monday, which is a public holiday. On that day it is traditional for people to go out into the country, fly kites and eat fasting foods. Two particularly popular places for this ritual, known as the *koúlouma*, are the Lássi peninsula and near Ámmes beach, near Svoronáta in the Livathó district.

The 25th of March is a red letter day on two counts: besides being the feast of the Annunciation, it marks the anniversary of the outbreak of the Greek Revolution against the Turks in 1821. Parades are held in all the towns and villages.

Easter, the greatest feast in the Christian liturgical calendar, is celebrated in Greece with many church services and all kinds of traditional observances. On Good Friday there is the *Epitáfios Thrínos* (Funerary Lament) in church, followed in the evening by a very moving procession in which the flower-covered bier is carried through the streets, followed by most of the local population holding lit candles. The Resurrection is celebrated at midnight on Holy Saturday and is greeted with firecrackers and sometimes fireworks. On Easter Sunday lambs are roasted whole on the spit, red-dyed hard-boiled eggs are eaten (having first been cracked in a traditional ritual) and the greeting *Christós Anésti* ('Christ is risen') is heard everywhere. May Day, the worldwide workers' festival, is also a celebration of spring: city-dwellers go out into the country for picnics and the front door of every house is decorated with a wreath of wild flowers.

On Kefaloniá, the union of the Ionian Islands with the rest of Greece (1864) is celebrated on 21st May with parades in the towns and the laying of wreaths. The 28th of October is a national holiday known as 'Óhi Day', because it commemorates the day in 1940 when the Greek government said 'No' to Mussolini's ultimatum and so entered the war against the forces of fascism. Not much notice is taken of birthdays in Greece, at least by adults. The normal practice is to celebrate one's name day, i.e. the feast-day of the saint whose name one bears (for most given names are saints' names). The commonest name in Kefaloniá is Yerásimos, whose feast-day is on 20th October. Other common names include Spíros (12th December), Dioníssis/Dionissía (17th December), Harálambos (10th February), Vangélis/Evangelía (25th March), Yeóryios/Yeoryía (23rd April), Konstandínos and Eléni (21st May) and Panayís/Panayóta/María (15th August). The standard greeting for a person on his or her name day is *Chrónia pollá* ('Many happy returns').

Family celebrations and religious festivals are great events in Greece and are welcomed as an excuse for dancing and feasting. The patronal feast-day of the local church is celebrated with a festival known as a *paniyíri*. In villages and at monasteries, if the patronal feast falls in summer, the *paniyíri* is held in the village square or the monastery courtyard, often after vespers on the eve of the feast-day. To make sure, ask at the place where you are staying. *Paniyíria* are always occasions of spontaneous merrymaking, with plenty of food, wine and dancing to live music. As often as not the village Cultural Society has a dance group which puts on a display of local dances, wearing traditional costume. If you go to a *paniyíri*, let yourself go and don't be shy about trying the Greek dances – not only with your friends but with Greeks you have never met before: they will be delighted if you join in. The next morning, the Divine Liturgy is celebrated in the flower-decked church. Many local traditions and customs are connected with the Orthodox faith.

Each municipal council issues leaflets giving details of the musical and theatrical performances, festivals and *paniyíria* scheduled for the summer season in its area. If you can't find a copy in your hotel or guesthouse, ask at a shop.

Travelling around the island

To explore Kefaloniá, a fairly large island, it is almost essential to have your own transport. Fortunately there are plenty of hire cars available. To hire a car you must be at least twenty-one years old. If you hire a motor scooter or motorbike, always wear a crash helmet (it is actually illegal to ride without one). Before setting out for the day, it is a good idea to study your route carefully on the map. The standard of signposting on the roads has improved greatly in recent years, and there are now signposts to all the beaches and many places of archaeological and historical interest. If you do get lost, don't be afraid to ask the way. Most people on the island, except the very old, speak English reasonably well.

The travel and tourist agencies sell tickets for one-day guided coach tours of the island and for one-day cruises to Itháki, which are very enjoyable.

Tavernas

In simple, traditional-style tavernas it is quite normal to go into the kitchen to choose the dishes one likes. At these places you will find only the standard Greek fare. In fish tavernas fresh fish is charged by the kilo: you choose your own fish from the refrigerator and it is then weighed in your presence. Restaurants in popular tourist resorts are more like their Western European counterparts and offer a choice of 'international' or Greek cuisine. Generally speaking, Greeks care more about good company and good food than up-market crockery and efficient service.

Zaharoplastía (patisseries, cake/confectionery shops)

The *zaharoplastío* is a familiar institution in Greece: you will usually find at least one in the main square of a small town and often in a village square. Besides traditional local confectioneries such as *amigdalópita* and *karidópita*, they offer sticky oriental sweets like *baklavá* and *kataífi* (with honey and almonds), chocolate and cream cakes, ice creams, toasted sandwiches, crystallized and candied fruits and yoghurt with honey. In summer the Greeks drink a lot of iced coffee (*kafé frappé*), which is made with instant coffee and served in a tumbler. When ordering, don't forget to specify how sweet you want it: *skéto* (neat) = no sugar; *métrio* (medium) = 1 tsp. sugar; *glikó* (sweet) = at least 2 tsp. sugar, e.g. *éna frappé métrio*. And the same applies to Greek coffee, which is very strong and is served in very small cups: e.g. *éna kafedáki métrio ellinikó* (one medium Greek coffee). If you want your iced coffee with milk, add the words *me gála*. Greek coffee is always served without milk. In most *zaharoplastía* you can also order cocktails and other alcoholic drinks.

Shops

In tourist resorts the shops stay open all day and until late in the evening. In small villages there is often only one small general store which frequently doubles as a café with a few tables and chairs.

Although the age of itinerant vendors is past, fishmongers and bakers still sometimes make their rounds in the villages. If you hear the cry *Frésko psári!* on a loudspeaker you will know that the fishmonger (or fisherman) is on his way. In summer itinerant greengrocers come over from the Peloponnese with vanloads of fruit and vegetables.

Kiosks (*períptera*)

A *períptero*, or pavement kiosk, crams an enormous range of stock into its tiny space: from newspapers and cigarettes to ice creams, toothpaste, films, soft drinks … you name it.

Banks and post offices

Opening hours: Banks 08:00-14:30 (Fridays 08:00-13:30). Post offices 07:30-14:00. All banks have ATMs (cash machines) which accept most credit cards. Stamps can also be bought at tourist shops and *períptera*.

Tourist Police

A Tourist Police service is offered at local police stations. In an emergency you can ring 171, a number which is valid from all over Greece and is on call 24 hours a day.

PRACTICAL INFORMATION

Useful phone numbers

Kefaloniá

Argostóli

Tourist Police	2671 023 226 or 171
G.N.T.O. (National Tourist Organization)	2671 022 248
Federation of Proprietors of Rented Rooms and Apartments in Kefaloniá and Itháki	2671 029 109
Prefecture	2671 022 120
Corgialenios Library	2671 028 221
Corgialenios Historical and Cultural Museum	2671 028 835
Fokás-Kosmetátos Foundation	2671 026 595
Argostóli Archaeological Museum	2671 028 300
Kefaloniá and Itháki Natural History Museum	2671 084 400
Ípiros Technical College, Agrobiology Dept.	2671 027 101
Ionian Islands Merchant Marine Academy	2671 028 608
Kefalonia and Ithaka Foundation	2671 025 550
A. Tritsis Foundation	2671 023 152
Historical Archives	2671 023 451
Argostóli Philharmonic School	2671 022 362
National Stadium	2671 028 528
Argostóli Sailing Club	2671 022 854
Harokópio Workshop	2671 028 794
Stevedores' Union	2671 028 117
Kefaloniá and Itháki Consumers' Association	2671 028 805
Association of Kefaloniá and Itháki Football Clubs	2671 024 789
Kefaloniá and Itháki Chamber of Commerce and Industry	2671 022 253
Technical Chamber of Greece	2671 026 840
Kefalonian Wine-Growers' Association	2671 026 878
Express Service	154
ELPA (Hellenic Automobile & Touring Club) breakdown service	104

Lixoúri

Ípiros Technical College, Musical Instrument Technology Dept.	2671 092 854
Public Library and Typáldos-Iakovátos Museum	2671 091 325
'Damodós' Petrítsios Public Library	2671 091 222
Lixoúri Philharmonic School	2671 092 386

Rest of Kefaloniá

Yeóryios and Máris Vergotís Cultural Centre	2671 041 155
Fiskárdo Nautical and Environmental Club	2674 041 181

Itháki

Vathí Maritime and Folk Art Museum	2674 033 398
Vathí Archaeological Museum	2674 032 200
Stavrós Archaeological Museum	2674 031 305
Vathí Public Library	2674 033 448
Centre for Homeric Studies	2107 273 560
Historical Archives	2674 032 719
Itháki Town Band	2674 033 251
Próödos Sports Club of Itháki	2674 033 484

Athens

Tourist Police	210 9242700 / 210 9243354 or 171
G.N.T.O. (National Tourist Organization)	210 3310565 / 210 3310692

Foreign embassies in Athens

Belgium	210 3617886-8
Canada	210 7273400
Cyprus	210 7237 883
Denmark	210 3608315-6
Finland	210 7519 795
France	210 7290154-6
Germany	210 7285 111
Irish Republic	210 7232771-2
Italy	210 7239 045
Netherlands	210 7239701-4
Sweden	210 7290 421
United Kingdom	210 7272 600
U.S.A.	210 7212951-9

e-mail

G.N.T.O. (National Tourist Organization)	eotda01@mail.otenet.gr
Prefecture of Kefaloniá and Itháki	nakefal@hol.gr
Municipality of Elios-Pronnoi	dimos@eleios-pronnoi.gr
Municipality of Sami	d-samis@otenet.gr
Municipality of Erissos	d-erisos@otenet.gr
Municipality of Ithaki	ithaki@otenet.gr
Corgialenios Library	korglib@otenet.gr
Corgialenios Historical and Cultural Museum	corgmuse@hol.gr
Fokás-Kosmetátos Foundation	ipfc@hol.gr
Central Public Library and Typáldos-Iakovátos Museum	library@compulink.gr
Fiskárdo Nautical and Environmental Club (FNEC)	fnec@otenet.gr
Kefalonian Wine-Growers' Association	valliang@otenet.gr
Agroindustrial Co-operative of Robóla Producers	robola@aias.gr
Yannikóstas Metaxás winery	metwines@kef.forthnet.gr
Gentilini winery	gentilini@compuserve.com
Vitorátos winery	vinvit@hol.gr

Websites

www.na-kefalinia.gr	Prefecture of Kefaloniá and Itháki
www.argostoli-mun.gr	Municipality of Argostóli
www.sami.gr	Municipality of Sámi
www.pylaros.gr	Municipality of Pílaros
www.elios-pronnoi.gr	Municipality of Eliós-Prónni
w www.kefalonia-ithaki.gr/corg	Corgialenios Library
www.culture.gr	Corgialenios Historical and Cultural Museum
	Argostóli Archaeological Museum
	Vathí Archaeological Museum
	Stavrós Archaeological Museum
www.aia.gr	Eleftherios Venizelos International Airport, Athens. Flight information, etc.
www.ktel.org	Bus companies. Timetable information
www.gnto.gr	G.N.T.O. (National Tourist Organization). Tourist information (general, Tourist Police, hotels, embassies, etc.)
www.gtp.gr	Greek Travel Pages. Information about public transport, ferry timetables, museums, hotels, etc.
www.ionion.com	Tourist guide to Kefaloniá and Itháki
www.kefalonia.net.gr	Tourist guide to Kefaloniá and Itháki
www.kefaloniathewaytogo.com	Tourist guide to Kefaloniá
www.fnec.gr	Fiskárdo Nautical and Environmental Club (FNEC)
www.elati.org	ELATI, a charity for the protection of the Énos wild horses. Plentiful information about the mountain and the horses
www.hellenic-cosmos.gr	Foundation of the Hellenic World. Greek history
www.robola.gr	Agroindustrial Co-operative of Robóla Producers

Travel agencies

KEFALONIA

A.D. TRAVEL	2671 093 142 adtravel@otenet.gr
AINOS TOURS	2671 022 333 ainos@otenet.gr
APHRO TRAVEL	2671 093 142 aphrotravel@ionion.com
C.B.R. TRAVEL	2671 022 770 cbr1@otenet.gr
CEFALONIA HOLIDAYS	2671 023 281 cefalonianholidays@ionion.com
CHELMIS TRAVEL	2671 025 400
ERTSOS W.T.S.	2671 027 301 travertso@kef.forthnet.gr
ETAM	2671 025 651 etam@compulink.gr
FILOXENOS	2671 023 055 filoxeno@otenet.gr
GEROLIMATOS TRAVEL	2674 061 036
GOULIMIS TOURS	2674 072 925
GREEK ISLANDS CLUB	2674 041 272
HOLIDAYS SERVICES	2671 023 737 eflagent@otenet,gr
KAVADAS TRAVEL	2674 072 750
KEFALONIA AGENCY	2671 027 333
KOKOLIS TRAVEL	2671 023 195 kokolis@otenet.gr
KTEL TOURS	2671 023 364
MAKI KEFALONIA HOLIDAYS	2674 072 365 maki@otenet.gr
MYRTOS	2671 025 023 myrtostr@hol.gr
NAUTILUS TRAVEL	2674 041 440
PANEM	2671 023 526
PERDIKIS TRAVEL	2671 092 503
PROPER KEFALONIAN	2671 026 924 info@pkt.gr
RALLATOS TRAVEL	2671 092 511 rallatos@hol.gr
ROMANOS TRAVEL	2671 023 541
SEAGULL HOLIDAYS	2674 072 001 seagull2@otenet.gr
SKALINA TOURS	2671 083 275 skalina@kef.forthnet.gr
SUNBIRD TRAVEL	2671 023 723

ITHÁKI

DELAS TOURS	2674 032 104 delas@otenet.gr
DIGALETOS	2674 031 762
GREEK ISLANDS CLUB	2764 031 076
POLYCTOR TOURS	2674 033 120

How to get to Kefaloniá and Itháki

By air
Athens - Kefaloniá
Zákinthos - Kefaloniá
And direct charter flights from various countries in Europe

By sea
From Pátra*
Pátra - Sámi - Vathí (Itháki)

From Killíni*
Killíni - Póros
Killíni - Argostóli

From Italy to Kefaloniá
Brindisi - Corfu - Sámi
From Italy to Kefaloniá via Pátra
Ancona - Pátra - Sámi
Venice - Pátra - Sámi

*Buses from Athens connect with the ferries.

Inter-island ferries

From Kefaloniá to Itháki
Sámi - Vathí
Sámi - Piso Aetós
**From Kefaloniá to Itháki
and Aitolo-Akarnanía**
Sámi - Piso Aetós - Astakós
From Kefaloniá to Zákinthos
Pessáda - Skinári
From Kefaloniá to Lefkáda
Fiskárdo - Vassilikí
Fiskárdo - Nidrí
From Kefaloniá to Corfu
Sámi - Corfu
From Itháki to Kefaloniá
Vathí - Sámi
Piso Aetós - Sámi
Fríkes - Fiskárdo

**From Itháki to Aitolo-Akarnanía
and Kefaloniá**
Piso Aetós - Astakós - Sámi
**From Itháki to Kefaloniá and
Lefkáda**
Fríkes - Fiskárdo - Vassilikí
From Zákinthos to Kefaloniá
Skinári - Pessáda
From Lefkáda to Itháki and Kefaloniá
Nidrí - Fríkes - Fiskárdo
From Corfu to Kefaloniá
Córfu - Sámi
**From Aitolo-Akarnanía to Kefaloniá
and Itháki**
Astakós - Sámi - Piso Aetós

Timetable information

Argostóli bus station	2671 022 281
Athens central bus station	2105 150 785
Olympic Airways, Argostóli	2671 028 808
Kefaloniá airport	2671 041 511
Eleftherios Venizelos International Airport, Athens	2103 530 000
Argostóli Port Authority	2671 022 224
Sámi Port Authority	2674 022 031
Póros Port Authority	2674 072 460
Itháki Port Authority	2674 032 909
Pátra Port Authority	2610 341 002
Killíni Port Authority	2623 092 211

And from the shipping companies' local offices

Hotels

KEFALONIÁ

ARGOSTÓLI DISTRICT

	ARGOSTÓLI	
AINOS	C	2671 028 013
ARGOSTOLI	C	2671 028 358
BYRON	C	2671 023 401
EVROPI	C	2671 024 681/2
FOKAS	C	2671 024 444
IONIAN PLAZA	C	2671 025 581/4
KASTELLO	C	2671 023 250/3
KEFALONIA STAR	C	2671 023 181/3
LOUKAS	C	2671 023 965/7
MIRABELLE	C	2671 025 381/3
MIRAMARE	C	2671 025 511/3
MIRAMARE II	C	2671 025 513
MOUIKIS	C	2671 023 454/6
OLGA	C	2671 024 981/4
TOURIST	C	2671 023 034

Hotels

ALLEGRO	D	2671 022 268
HARA	D	2671 022 427
PARTHENON	D	2671 022 246

LÁSSI		
MÉDITERRANÉE	A	2671 028 760/3
PRINCESS	B	2671 025 591/2
IRILENA	C	2671 023 172
LASSI	C	2671 023 126
LORENZO	C	2671 028 783

| **PLATÍS YALÓS** | | |
| WHITE ROCKS | A | 2671 028 332/5 |

FANÁRI		
FANARI	C	2671 022 324
GALAXIAS	C	2671 024 096

LIXOURI DISTRICT

LIXOÚRI		
LA CITÉ	C	2671 092 701
PALATINO	C	2671 092 780
POSEIDON	C	2671 092 518
SUMMERY	C	2671 091 771

| **KOUNÓPETRA** | | |
| IONIAN SEA | B | 2671 092 280 |

| **MÉGAS LÁKKOS** | | |
| CEPHALONIAN BEACH | C | 2671 092 679 |

| **ÁYIOS DIMÍTRIOS** | | |
| TERRA MARE | C | 2671 092 360 |

| **AMMOÚSSA** | | |
| AMMOUSSA | C | 2671 094 354 |

| **XI** | | |
| CEPHALONIA PALACE | A | 2671 092 555 |

LIVATHÓ DISTRICT

| **AYÍA PELAYÍA** | | |
| IRINA | B | 2671 041 285/7 |

| **VLAHÁTA** | | |
| MARIA-ANNA | C | 2671 031 171 |

| **KARAVÁDOS** | | |
| KARAVADOS BEACH | B | 2671 069 400 |

| **KORIÁNNA** | | |
| KEFALONIA SUN | C | 2671 069 651 |

| **KOUNDOURÁTA** | | |
| SUNRISE INN | B | 2671 069 586 |

| **KOURKOUMELÁTA** | | |
| KOURKOUMELATA | C | 2671 041 151 |

Hotels

	LOURDÁTA	
LARA	C	2671 031 157
	TRAVLIÁTA	
IONIS	C	2671 069 322
	SPARTIÁ	
PANAS	B	2671 069 506
	SVORONÁTA	
AMMES	B	2671 041 809
BLUE HORIZON	B	2671 041 177/8
	TRAPEZÁKI	
TRAPEZAKI BAY	C	2671 031 502

ELIÓS-PRÓNNI DISTRICT

	SKÁLA	
APOSTOLATA-LOUIS RESORT	A	2671 083 581/2
ASTERIS	A	2671 083 021
PELAGOS BAY	A	2671 083 603
SAN GIORGIO	A	2671 083 267
ALIKI	B	2671 083 427/8
9 MUSSES	B	2671 083 560
MAREL	B	2671 083 427/8
MARINA BAY	B	2671 083 592
MOUNDA BEACH	B	2671 083 151/3
PORTO SKALA	B	2671 083 501/6
CAPTAIN'S HOUSE	C	2671 083 389
MARIETTA	C	2671 083 141
OCEAN VIEW	C	2671 083 391
PASPALIS	C	2671 083 140
POSEIDON	C	2671 083 431/2
SKALA	C	2671 083 202
STAR LIGHT	C	2671 083 436
TARA BEACH	C	2671 083 250
NATALIE	D	2671 083 190

	PÓROS	
ODYSSEYS PALACE	A	2674 072 036
BELVEDERE	B	2674 072 493/4
FILOXENIA	C	2674 072 926/7
KEFALOS	C	2674 072 139/41
KRISTI	C	2674 072 569
LOUIZA	C	2674 072 571/2
MAKEDONIA	C	2674 072 814
MICHAELA	C	2674 072 314
OCEANIS	C	2674 072 581/2
POROS BAY	C	2674 072 594/5
GALINI	E	2674 072 353
POROS HOUSE	E	2674 072 417
RIVIERA	E	2674 072 327

SÁMI DISTRICT

SÁMI DISTRICT		
PERIKLES	B	2674 022 780/5
SAMI BEACH	B	2674 022 824
THODORA	B	2674 022 650
IONION	C	2674 022 035

Hotels

KASTRO	C	2674 022 656
KYMA	D	2674 022 064
MELISSANI	D	2674 022 464
KARAVÓMILOS		
ATHINA	C	2674 022 779

PÍLAROS DISTRICT

AYÍA EFIMÍA		
GONATAS	B	2674 061 213
APHRODITI	C	2674 061 113
BOULEVARD	C	2674 061 800
LOGARA	C	2674 061 202
MOUSTAKIS	C	2674 061 030

ÉRISSOS DISTRICT

FISKÁRDO		
ERISSOS	A	2674 041 055
FILOXENIA	A	2674 041 410
ODYSSEAS	B	2674 051 315
STELLA	B	2674 041 211
KAMINAKIA	C	2674 041 218
PANORMOS	C	2674 041 203
ANTIPÁTA		
DAFNOUDI	C	2674 041 279
VILLA HARA	C	2674 051 343
MATSOUKÁTA		
ALEXANNA	C	2674 041 293

ITHÁKI

VATHÍ		
MENTOR	B	2674 033 033
KAPETAN YANNIS	C	2674 033 311
ODYSSEYS	C	2674 032 381
OMIRIKON		2674 033 596/8
FRÍKES		
NOSTOS	C	2674 031 644
KIÓNI		
KIONI	B	2674 031 789

Camping sites in Kefaloniá

FANÁRI	
ARGOSTOLI BEACH	2671 023 487
SÁMI	
KARAVOMILOS	2674 022 480

Books on Kefalonia in English

Cephalonia - Ecclesiastical Art, vols. I-III, published by the Society for Historical Research on Cephalonia.

Dedication to the National Park of Ainos, published by the Museum of Natural History, Cephalonia and Ithaca, Argostóli 1998.

Marinatos, Spyros, *A Short Historical and Archaeological Sketch*, published by the Corgialenios Historical and Cultural Museum, Argostóli 1962.

Odysseas, lavishly illustrated cultural magazine with English summaries of the Greek text. Argostóli 1999, 2000, 2001.

Several books on the history of Kefaloniá have been published in English and can be bought in the shop of the Corgialenios Historical and Cultural Museum, Argostóli.

INDEX

A

Acqui Division 27, 57
Aetós, acropolis, 155
Aetós, isthmus, 153
Afálon Bay 172
Aínos: see Énos
Ái-Yánnis170
Akrotíri 133
Alalkomenai 155
Andipáta, Érissos, 115
Andipáta, Pílaros, 112
Andreoláta 85
Androútsos, O., 157
Annináta 85
Ánninos, A., 68
Anoyí 169
Antípas, M., 26, 112
Argaliós hill 173
Argostóli 13, 46, 48
Aryínia 83
Asproyérakas 85
Ássos 114, 116
Athéras 17
Atsoupádes 83
Ávithos, Lake, 91
Ayía Dinatí, Mt., 111
Ayía Efimía 108
Ayía Iríni 85
Ayía Thékli 137
Áyii Fanéndes, monastery, 99
Áyii Saránda 172
Áyii Theódori, lighthouse, 56
Áyios Athanásios 171
Áyios Dimítrios 126
Áyios Nikólaos 91
Áyios Yeóryios 84
Áyios Yeóryios, chapel, 82

B

Barbarossa, Khair-ed-Din, 19
Beaches
    Ái-Hélis 63
    Ámmes 63
    Andíssamos 101
    Áspros Yalós 170
    Ávithos 63
    Ayía Eléni 136
    Ayía Ierousalím 115
    Ayía Kiriakí 126
    Ayía Paraskeví 104
    Áyios Thomás 70
    Dexá 166
    Émblisi 115
    Fanári 56

Filiatró 165
Fóki 115
Kalámia 60
Kamínia 80
Katsikoúli 173
Koróni 79
Koumariá 124
Kourvoúlia 173
Langadákia 135
Lépeda 132
Liménia, Itháki, 173
Liménia, Kefaloniá, 87
Lourdás 77
Loútsa 165
Makriá Pétra 87
Makrís Yalós 57
Mbros Aetós 167
Mégas Lákkos 133
Mírtos 113
Mnímata 165
Petaní 137
Plakoútses 173
Platiá Ámmos 136
Platís Yalós 57
Potamákia 80
Ráyia 87
Sarakinári 173
Sarakíniko 165
Skála 81
Skíno 165
Sotíra 124
Trapezáki 77
Tsirimbí 165
Xi 133
Yidáki 165
Bérard, V., 157
Bernières, L. de, 101
Bonános, Y., 134
Bosset, C.P. de, 46
Byron, Lord, 65, 67

C

Capes, J., 80
Castles (Venetian)
    Ássos 114, 116
    St. George (Kástro) 18, 21, 68, 69
Caves
    Angaláki 98
    Ayía Eleoússa 98
    Áyii Theódori 98
    Drákena 15, 85
    Drongaráti 97
    Hiridóni 98
    Loízou 154, 171

188

Marmarospiliá (Cave of the Nymphs) 166
Melissáni 28, 101, 102
St. Gerasimos 58
Zerváti 98
Churches
  Ayía Efimía 108
  Ayía Marína 132
  Ayía Paraskeví 77
  Ayía Varvára 94
  Áyii Apóstoli 134, 135
  Áyios Elefthérios 92
  Áyios Harálambos 132
  Áyios Nikólaos, Argostóli, 51
  Áyios Nikólaos, Mavrónas (Itháki), 173
  Áyios Nikólaos, Sámi, 99
  Áyios Nikólaos, Vathí, 164
  Áyios Nikólaos, Vátsa (Palikí), 134
  Áyios Spirídon, Argostóli, 50
  Áyios Spirídon, Pouláta, 97
  Áyios Yeóryios, Kondoyenáda, 137
  Áyios Yeóryios, Skála, 82
  Evangelístria, Farakláta, 94
  Evangelístria, Kástro, 79
  Kímisis tis Theotókou, Rónghi (Palikí), 136
  Panayía, Anoyí (Itháki), 169
  Panayía, Convent of Áyios Yerásimos, 139
  Panayía, Días islet, 63
  Panayía Fidoússa 83
  Panayía Sissiótissa 49
  Panayía tis Perlingoú 132
  Presentation of the Blessed Virgin, Vathí, 164
  Profítis Ilías, Kióni (Itháki), 173
  SS Constantine and Helena 70
  Sotíras, Stavrós (Itháki), 170
  Sotíras, Vathí, 163
  Theotókos, Sámi, 100
Corfu: see Kérkira
Crete 19, 22
Cultural Centres
  Fiskárdo Nautical and Environmental Club 119
  Itháki Cultural Centre 164
  Kateliós Environmental and Cultural Centre 80
  Metaxáta Cultural Centre 64
Cyprus 19

D
Damodós, V. 22, 135
Damoulianáta 136
Defaranáta 114
Demoutsandáta 141
Dendrináta 112
Días islet 63
Digalétto 91
Dilináta 94
Divaráta 113
Domáta 63
Dorizáta 70
Dörpfeld, W., 149, 157

Doúri Hill 127
Dracoulis, P., 165
Drakáta 110
Drakopouláta 110
Drápanos bridge 46
Drápanos cemetery 52

E
Echinádes 153
Eliós district 15, 79
Eliós-Prónni, municipality, 13
Énos (Aínos), Mt., 13, 28, 29, 142
Eptánisa (Heptanese, Seven Islands) 13, 22
Érissos 13, 114
Evmorfía, Mt. 46
Évyeros, Mt., 46
Exoyí 172

F
Faniés 85
Farakláta 94
Fársa 124
Favatáta 135
Ferendináta 19
Fiskárdo 15, 115
Fourniá peninsula 119
Fríkes 172
Fuca, Juan de, 34

G
Gell, W., 157
Gentili, A., 23
Gerásimos, St., 58, 139
Gladstone, W., 26
Goekoop, A., 65, 157
Grizáta 92
Guiscard, R., 17

H
Halikerá 66
Haliotáta 97
Harákti 91
Harálambos, St., 132
Havdáta 135
Havriáta 135
Hionáta 79
Homer 146

I
Ikonómou, F., 157
Ikosimía district 76
Iliad 146
Ionian Academy 25
Ionian Islands 13, 19, 20
Ionian Sea 13
Ionian State 23, 25
Istrati, Panait, 95
Ithakos 154

K
Kálamos 172
Kaláta 137
Kalligás, P., 66
Kalligáta 63
Kalón Óros 112
Kambánas, Platía, 23, 51
Kambitsáta 85
Kaminaráta 135
Kapandríti 85
Kapodístrias, I., 130
Karavádos 70
Karavómilos 28, 101
Kardakáta 124
Kariá 114
Kástro 68
Katavóthres 56
Kateliós 80
Kavvadías, N., 49
Kavvadías, P., 67
Kéfalos Theatre 49
Kephallenia 15-16
Kephalos 16
Keramiés 70
Kérkira (Corfu) 13, 20
Kióni 173
Kíthira (Kythera) 13
Klísmata 70
Kokoláta 66
Kolierí 172
Kolónas, L., 86
Komitáta 112
Kondogouráta 124
Kondoyenáda 137
Konidaráta 114
Koriánna 70
Kothréas 114
Koulouráta 92
Kounópetra (rocking-stone) 133
Kourkoumeláta 63
Kouroukláta 124
Koútavos lagoon 46, 52
Koutroukói 85
Kouvaláta 126
Krane 16, 96
Kraniá 15
Krassás, S., 68
Kyatis, acropolis, 99

L
Lahós 172
Lakíthra 66, 67
Laskarátos, A., 126, 131
Lássi 56
Lavrángas, D., 96
Lazarétto islet 163
Leake, W.M., 156, 157
Lefkáda (Leukas) 13
Léfki 170

Libraries
Corgialenios 53
Damodós 131
Iakovátios 130
Lihoúdis brothers 22, 34
Livadás, Y., 25
Livádi plain 126
Livathó district 13. 15, 62
Lixoúri 127
Lourdáta 77

M
Maitland, T., 23
Makriótika 111
Mandoukáta 135
Mánganos 115
Manzavináta 132
Marathiás 166
Margaritone 18
Marinátos, S., 67, 137
Markópoulo 83
Matsoukáta 115
Mavráta 79
Mavrónas Bay 173
Mazarakáta 68
Mazarakáta, archaeological site, 66
Merovígli, Mt., Itháki, 166
Merovígli, Mt., Kefaloniá, 124
Mesovoúnia 114
Mesovounó 172
Metaxás brothers 24
Metaxáta 63, 66
Miniátis, I., 129
Miniés 62
Mitakáta 141
Molféttas, Y., 130
Mólos, Gulf of, 153, 162
Momferátos, I., 25
Monasteries and Convents
Áyios Andréas Milapidiás 67
Áyios Yerásimos 139
Katharón 169
Kechriónos 127
Kipouréon 136
Koronáton 135
Paliohérsou 114
Panayía Agrilíon 101
Síssia 77
Taxiarchón 166
Themáton 112
Theotókos Átrou 88
Zoödóhos Piyí 83
Monopoláta 136
Móskos, I., 22
Moúnda, Cape, 80, 81
Moussáta 77
Museums
Archaeological, Argostóli 53
Archaeological, Stavrós 171

Archaeological, Vathí 164
Corgialenios Historical and Cultural 54
Ecclesiastical, Convent of Áyios Andréas
Milapidiás 67
Fokás-Kosmetátos 54
House of the Owls and Hedgehogs 70
Kefaloniá and Itháki Natural History 54
Maritime and Folk Art, Vathí 164
Radio and Telecommunications Equipment 54
Traditional Arts and Crafts, Kaminaráta 135
Traditional Arts and Crafts, Platrithiás 172
Typáldos-Iakovátos 130

N
Napier, C., 24
Neohóri 112
Nífi 124
Nírito, Mt., 153

O
Odysseus 15, 147
Odyssey 147
Omalá valley 13, 139
Orsini, M., 18

P
Paízis, T., 157
Pakhní, acropolis, 87
Pale 16
Paleohóra 166
Palikí district 13, 15, 124
Paliókastro, acropolis of Same (Sámi), 99
Pakhní, acropolis (Póros), 87
Paliókastro, acropolis of Pronnoi (Pástra), 84
Panás, E., 24, 70
Panormos 16, 17
Papadópoulos, I., 158
Partsch, J., 144
Pástra 83
Patrikáta 114
Paxí 13
Peloponnese 15
Perahóri 166
Péra Pigádi islet 166
Pernarákia 172
Pessáda 70
Petrikáta 124
Petrítsis, S., 129
Philharmonic School, Lixoúri, 132
Pílaros district 13, 108
Pilikáta 154, 171
Piryí 91
Píso Aetós 167
Platiés 79
Platrithiás 172
Playiá 114
Pólis Bay 154, 171
Póros 15, 85

Poulákis, T., 22
Pouláta 97
Prónni/Pronnoi 15, 16, 84, 143
Pterelaos 16

R
Radicals 25, 51
Radzaklí 80
Razáta 95
Rífi 136
Rónghi 136
Roúdi, Mt., 144, 145

S
Sámi /Same 13, 15, 16, 97, 98, 99
Sarláta 63
Schliemann, H., 149, 158
Seaton, Lord, 25
Septinsular Republic 23
Simeónoglou, S., 158
Simotáta 77
Skála 15, 25, 81
Skála, Roman villa, 82
Skarlátos, P., 132
Skiniá 137
Soldáto Castle 92
Soullári 132
Spartiá 70
Spathí 85
Stavrós 170, 171
Svoronáta 63

T
Tafíon, monastery, 136
Taphios 16
Theme of Kephallenia 17
Thiniá district 124
Thirámona 79
Tocchi family 18
Travliáta 68
Trítsis, A., 52
Troianáta 141
Tsakarissiáno 91
Tselendáta 115
Tsitsélis, I., 135
Typáldos-Iakovátos, Y., 25
Tzamareláta 114
Tzanetáta 92
Tzangarólas, S., 22
Tzannáta 85
Tzannáta, Mycenaean tholos tomb, 15, 86

V
Valeriáno 79
Valeriános Fokás, A., 34
Valliános, P., 70
Valliánou, Platía 49
Valsamáta 139

Vardiáni islet 133
Varí 114
Vassilikádes 114
Vassilopouláta 110
Vathí 153, 162
Vátsa 133
Venice 18, 20, 22
Vergotís, Y., 63
Vilatória 137
Vlaháta 77
Vouní 134

W
Warnecke, H., 16
Wineries
    Agroindustrial Co-operative of Robóla
Producers 141
        Gentilini 62

Hartouliáris 70
Sklávos 127
Vitorátos 133
Yannikóstas Metaxás 80

X
Xenópoulo 85

Y
Yerákis, K., 35
Yerásimos, St.: see Gerásimos
Yero-gómbos, lighthouse, 135

Z
Zákinthos (Zante) 13, 15
Zerváta 92
Zervós-Iakovátos, I., 25
Zóla 126